The Surpassing Greatness
Of Christ

The Surpassing Greatness of Christ

IN HIM IS LIFE,
AND THAT LIFE IS THE LIGHT
OF HUMANITY.

Graeme Schultz

Gobsmacked Publishing

All Scripture quotations, unless otherwise indicated, are taken from the Holy Bible, New International Version®, NIV®. Copyright ©1973, 1978, 1984, 2011 by Biblica, Inc.™ Used by permission of Zondervan. All rights reserved worldwide. www.zondervan.com The "NIV" and "New International Version" are trademarks registered in the United States Patent and Trademark Office by Biblica, Inc.™

Copyright © 2017 Graeme Schultz.

All rights reserved. No part of this publication may be reproduced, distributed or transmitted in any form or by any means, including photocopying, recording, or other electronic or mechanical methods, without the prior written permission of the publisher, except in the case of brief quotations embodied in critical reviews and certain other noncommercial uses permitted by copyright law. For permission requests, write to the publisher, addressed "Permissions Coordinator," at the address below.

Graeme Schultz/Gobsmacked Publishing

19 Trotters Lane,
Cudgee, Victoria, Australia, 3265.

Ordering Information:
www.gobsmackedpublishing.com.au

National Library of Australia Cataloguing-in-Publication Entry

Creator: Schultz, Graeme, author.

Title: The Surpassing Greatness of Christ; In Him Was Life, And That Life Is The Light Of Humanity/Graeme Schultz.

ISBN: 9780994603043 (paperback)

9780994603050 (ebook)

Subjects: Christian life. Spiritual life–Christianity. God–Knowableness. God–Love.

Dedicated to the 'one'...

– Jesus Christ, who lives in me –

Contents

Author's note ix

Introduction 1

Chapter 1 Did You Know? 3

Chapter 2 I Am the Truth 7

Chapter 3 That I May Know Christ 9

Chapter 4 Lost For Words 13

Chapter 5 New Doors 17

Chapter 6 Letting God Love Me 21

Chapter 7 Trusting in His Word 27

Chapter 8 The Living Word – In Me 35

Chapter 9 A Deeper Look 39

Chapter 10 The Kingdom of God 43

Chapter 11 In The Beginning Was the Word 47

Chapter 12 How Far Do We Go? 51

Chapter 13 I No Longer Live, But Christ Lives in Me 55

Chapter 14 The Divine Operating System 59

Chapter 15 The Father's Heart 63

Chapter 16 Participating in the Divine Nature 69

Chapter 17 Seeing the World as God Sees It 75

Chapter 18 Living in Eternity, While on Earth 79

Chapter 19 God Is My Home 83

Chapter 20 A Marriage Made in Heaven 87

Chapter 21 Learning How to be Loved by God 93

Chapter 22 Let the Celebrations Begin 97

Chapter 23 The Bride of Eternity 103

Chapter 24 The Surpassing Greatness of Christ 109

Conclusion 113

Author's note

My intention in writing this book has been to 'express the in-expressible', the most astonishing spectacle ever presented to humanity – the surpassing greatness of Christ.

Christianity is not primarily about the programs, activities and causes of church life, it is about the union that Jesus re-built between us and God. I spent the better part of my life deeply involved in the organization that represents the Lord of Glory, but the busyness of church life had a way of filtering out the magnificence of what I was actually in. I participated in the whole thing - except for the thing that matters most; the inexpressible wonder of knowing Christ Jesus.

Now at last I know what I was missing, so I invite you to come on a journey with me into Christ. Not so that we can be better equipped for ministry, or more successful in our area of service – but because he is the lover of our souls, and he wants us to sit still and let him love us.

I have deliberately written in a way that is more conversational than instructional. My intention in this conversation is not to tell you how to think or believe; only you can do that.

But I am certain that once Jesus has been seen for who he really is, it will render you speechless too – unable to describe the indescribable... *and you will be profoundly changed forever.*

Introduction

This is the third book in the 'Born of God' trilogy. In the second book I described a lie that was written into the fallen nature of humanity, it is a lie that seems so right that we don't question its validity – with the result that we have difficulty grasping the thing we want most - to 'walk in the Spirit'.

The lie that is written into the Old Nature is erased from our lives when we take hold of the truth that is written into our New Nature.

The truth that is written into our New Nature is so stunning and far-reaching in its potential to transform us that it renders the old lie ridiculous – yet the lie continues to persist and hamper Christians, because it is so established in our thinking.

In John 6:63 Jesus put the comparison between the truth and the lie out there for the world to see; "The Spirit gives life, the flesh counts for nothing".

We know that the flesh harbors a lie, but what we fail to appreciate - is that it tells this lie to itself. It is a self-perpetuating lie that we inadvertently repeat to ourselves over and over again – and it obscures something that is so spectacular by comparison that the angels in heaven must be scratching their heads in wonder – *they have been given the Spirit / but they choose the flesh instead.*

I spent much of the previous book exposing the nature of the flesh. It was my attempt to show that we validate the flesh in our attempts to present God with a lifestyle of good deeds and religious activities. While these are not bad in themselves, they have distracted us from something that is so superior in comparison that it renders them trite – *the magnificence of 'Christ in me'.*

I won't direct a lot of my focus onto 'the flesh' in this book; instead I will swing my gaze across to the most astonishing spectacle ever presented to humanity – the surpassing greatness of Christ.

If you are looking for tips on maintaining the presence of God, or principles for walking in God's favor and blessing, you won't find them in these pages. Yet it is my conviction that goodness and mercy will follow us all the days of our life, as we allow ourselves to be captivated by the spectacle which is 'Christ and Him crucified'.

This is not so much an academic exercise, or another subject for our meditation – rather it is the same magnificent obsession that consumed the Apostle Paul and overwhelmed his existence to the point of rapture. To discover the extravagance of Christ became his sole objective; and the more he discovered, the more wide-eyed and awe-struck he became.

Paul was not an isolated case, others throughout history have also glimpsed the breath-taking spectacle of Christ – it is available to us all, if we will only let go of our dependence on our self-made worth.

My hope, and indeed my passion; is that as the *'age before* Christ *returns'* nears its conclusion, we will see a spectacle never before seen in history – multitudes upon multitudes of people who have viewed Christ in a new way, and lost themselves in the staggering mystery of his grandeur and love.

Chapter 1
Did You Know?

Did you know that Christ is better at holding you in your salvation – than satan is at robbing you of it?

Did you know that God saw the rebellion of satan coming, and planned our salvation even before satan challenged God for the top job?

Did you know that God saw your life even before satan rebelled; he saw your face, your personality, and your intellect – he knew all your human weaknesses and strengths, and he crafted a salvation so robust that even our human foolishness was no match for it.

In God's mind you were saved even before you were born... *and long before you sinned!*

God anticipated everything, every dumb thought, word, and deed we could produce – and he set about saving us from ourselves, *in spite of ourselves.*

Jesus is "The Lamb that was slain before the world began" *(according to Revelations 13:8)*. As far as God was concerned, Jesus had been sent to die for us, before Adam breathed his first breath. The clock which defines human history had not even started to tick... yet the eternal mind of God had resolved our plight *(before we even had a plight)* – all that remained was for the timeline of human history to come into alignment with the heart of God.

Did you know that God created you *'with the potential to sin'* quite deliberately?

He didn't create us to <u>be</u> sinners - but the potential was always there.

It was not a mistake or a slip-up in our design. It wasn't even that satan caught everyone off guard, and tricked them before they realized what was happening. God knew Adam and Eve would sin and he didn't for a moment consider re-engineering them, so that it wouldn't happen.

He did this because the characteristic which caused Adam and Eve to separate themselves from God all those years ago in the garden, was the very same characteristic that connects us with God's heart as we return again. He wants us to freely choose His Love, His Life, and His Nature.

He placed the two trees side by side in the middle of the Garden of Eden. The Tree of Life / and the Tree of the Knowledge of Good and Evil, were equally available to Adam and Eve. God never considered hiding the bad tree out the back *where they might miss it.* He would never obstruct their ability to choose. In fact he valued their ability to choose so highly that he decided to send Jesus to die, rather than meddle with our free will.

All of this he saw in advance, and he went ahead anyway.

The deceit of satan was that he got Adam and Eve thinking about what it would be like to produce worth from their own means - *instead of receiving it from God.* It was the same notion that was behind satan's own rebellion; *they could take over the top job – they could be god for themselves.*

Sadly the human race began a quest they were never designed for, to generate <u>*from within themselves*</u> the life of happiness and fulfillment that we all crave. We were designed by God for that happiness and fulfillment to flow naturally out of our union with God, but we opted instead to set-about constructing it from our own deeds.

As long as Adam and Eve chose to dine on the Tree of Life they enjoyed a holy innocence, it was how God made them – he built into them an appetite for Life, an appetite that he satisfied freely as his divine nature flowed through them - *because it was his nature to do so.* He made them in his own image as people who reveled in a love relationship with no strings attached – people who would choose to be sustained by that love, rather than be constrained within it.

> ***This love relationship with 'no strings attached' is the reason why Christ came.***

If we do not have a profound understanding of this truth, then our Christianity will be stunted and never grow to real maturity. There is no meaning to be found in any Christian activity / if we have not first hidden ourselves in the truth that God loves us quite apart from what we do *(good and bad)* - and that he set-about making us his own before we even needed to be rescued from our foolish mistakes.

Perhaps the most tragic fallout caused by Adam's departure from the presence of God, is that we seem to have lost the ability to let God love us.

God created us with the expressed purpose that we would be the objects of his love, we *(the human race)* were created with an insatiable appetite for the unconditional love of God; it was written into our spiritual DNA – yet we opted out... for a love with strings attached. These strings were dependent on *our* ability to present God with a pleasing life.

The veil of the flesh hid Adams eyes *(and all of us that followed)* from the real truth, God's love could not be thwarted by the foolishness of man. Even though humanity abandoned it's true spiritual DNA and chose a self-made version, God would remain true to himself and love us unconditionally for all eternity.

We may well have remade our nature to look to ourselves for our sense of worth - but that didn't mean that God fell in step with us, and re-tuned his nature to suit us.

There is a curious verse in Romans 8:19 "For the creation waits in eager expectation for the children of God to be revealed" – we are revealed as 'God's children' to all of creation, when we finally stop trying so hard - and simply let God love us.

As we go forward through the pages and chapters that follow, I would like to unpack the scandalous notion that God wants to love us, he wants to give us life, and he wants to lift us up - more than our wildest imaginings, *more even than our own hearts hope for.* He has no agenda but to lavish his unsearchable love on us, and the only thing that inhibits his longing is our determination to have his love on our terms, instead of his.

God will not remake his gospel to suit our compulsion to come to him clothed in the garb of religion and lifestyle. He made us naked of self-made worth *(it was how he formed us to be)* – and this nakedness allowed the righteous heart of God to clothe us. It was free, it was abundant, and it was as natural as breathing – we *the human race,* were designed to be vessels into which God poured his goodness, 24/7.

This book is my attempt to reveal God; his love, his nature, his heart - as Adam and Eve knew him six thousand years ago, *before they walked away.* My hope is that our experiment with 'man-focused' religion will fade from view as we cast our eyes over the magnificent spectacle which is 'Christ and him crucified'.

Chapter 2
I Am the Truth

Jesus gave himself the title 'The Truth' in John 14:6; Jesus answered, "I am the way and the truth and the life. No one comes to the Father except through me". He was making a motherhood statement that defined his being – much as *'God is Love' defines his Father's being.*

Jesus was saying more than "I always tell the truth, or I can show you the truth, or even I am best at revealing the truth". He was saying that he is 'The Truth' – the absolute truth, the greatest truth, even the only truth.

Jesus was not saying that there were many truths, and if stood side-by-side he was the greatest one – he was saying that he is the origin, the center, and the substance of all truth.

It is this understanding that enables us to gain a proper perspective as we lead our complex and busy lives as Christians in this modern age. We have become so deeply engaged in such a vast array of activities, causes and programs that they have become our 'truth'. Sure we give a polite nod to Christ and thank him for kick-starting the whole thing, but then we refocus on the *'real'* stuff of Christianity and turn our gaze away from Mr. Truth himself.

It is a classic 'elephant in the room' situation – Christ looms so overwhelmingly large over the whole landscape of our faith – but we barely know how to acknowledge him. Sure we worship him, discuss him, we speculate about his plans and purposes, but we have lost the knack for being 'in him'.

So our Christianity has devolved into an exercise of human involvement in the activities of his movement, instead of a daily walk in the wonder of his love.

But what would such a walk look like – and how would it differ from what we are doing now?

To know that, we must re-discover the truth of him!

To do that we must make a quantum shift in our thinking – we must re-elevate Christ to his place as supreme and absolute truth. Not the things we do in response to him, or the habits and rituals that we have established which define our faith... *but Jesus himself – we must calm-down and let him be himself in us.*

I've been around Christianity for a long time. I've heard the preaching, attended the bible studies, and joined-in with the discussions – and my observation after all this time is that we are strong on our response to God, and weak on our understanding of his heart toward us.

**We know what to do
– but we don't know how to be.**

It is exactly the same problem that got Adam off the tracks in the first place – we were designed to 'be' first, and then the 'doing' took care of itself. It was the overflow – but we choose to focus on the 'doing', with the result that we become so 'self-conscious' that there was no room left... *for God to fill with himself.*

By now you may have a feeling where this is heading; maybe you are even starting to squirm a little as your established thought-processes rise-up in defense, if that is the case I would ask that you be patient with me. I would ask that you settle yourself, and take the risk of coming with me on a journey into Christ.

Chapter 3
That I May Know Christ

Philippians 3:10 "I want to know Christ and the power of His resurrection and the fellowship of His sufferings, being conformed to Him in His death".

This was a scripture that I kept a wide berth of for most of my life. I wanted to know Christ and the power of his resurrection – but I didn't want to fellowship in his sufferings and be conformed to his death.

It was the stuff of pain and suffering *(and even death)*, Paul seemed to be saying "bring it on" – *but I wasn't interested in going there.*

My problem was that I had been reading this scripture through the lens of '*doing*' instead of '*being*'. I had my eyes fixed on the natural consequences and not the spiritual reality. Paul wasn't actually saying "bring on the pain and death" he was saying "bring on more and more of Christ".

If we go back a bit, we read in verse 8 these words; "I consider everything a loss compared to the surpassing greatness of <u>knowing</u> Christ Jesus my Lord". He didn't say that "he considered everything a loss compared to the surpassing greatness of <u>serving</u> Christ Jesus my Lord" because he knew that 'serving Jesus' bubbled-up out of 'knowing him'. But without knowing him, his service was no more than the compulsions of an overactive conscience.

Paul saw something in the sufferings and death of Christ that I didn't. It was much deeper than the event that took place on the visible theatre of life on planet earth, and Paul considered every other endeavor a loss - that he may know this one thing.

If it was good enough for Paul, then it is good enough for me – *but what could it be that Paul knew?*

I have noticed that every time Paul speaks of the greatness of Christ he seems to become lost for words. As he attempts to contain Christ within his everyday language he finds it inadequate for the task, and so he gropes around to find expressions and superlatives that are able to do the job. In the end he is at a loss to describe the indescribable, as evidenced in his letters to the Ephesians and others.

Ephesians 1:19 "and his <u>incomparably</u> great power for us who believe".

Ephesians 1:23 "the <u>fullness</u> of him who <u>fills everything</u> in <u>every way</u>".

Ephesians 2:7 "in order that in the coming ages he might show the <u>incomparable</u> riches of his grace".

Ephesians 3:8 "the <u>unsearchable</u> riches of Christ".

Ephesians 3:16 "I pray that out of his <u>glorious riches</u>…"

Ephesians 3:18 "to grasp how <u>wide and long and high and deep</u> is the love of Christ".

Ephesians 3:19 "and to know this love that <u>surpasses</u> knowledge".

Ephesians 3:20 "Now to him who is able to do <u>immeasurably</u> more than all we can ask or imagine".

Then he continues in a number of verses in both Ephesians and Colossians to introduce yet another new concept 'the mystery of Christ'.

There was a time when I considered Paul to be a difficult fellow – a bit like Jonah only eight centuries later. He seemed to always be cranky about something, if it wasn't the poor old Galatians; it was Jews, or women, or anyone who stepped in his way. But I get it now; he had seen the wonder of Christ and it made the practice of mere religion intolerable.

I wonder what he would be cranky about if he came in to some of our meetings.

Would he say to us "you have contained the uncontainable, in your structures, programs & doctrines"? Would he say "take a step back from all your busyness (consider it rubbish, that you might know Christ)"? Or perhaps "you have turned Christ into a mission statement - when he is a person who lives in your heart".

I have heard that when Brother Yun from China and others who have discovered Christ without the trappings of western religion come to visit a western church for the first time – they are staggered that so much of what we do is so irrelevant in the context of the greatness of Christ.

It not my intention to labor the shortcomings of western Christianity – but it is good to contemplate the possibility that there is another way to be Christian that better reflects the sentiments of Paul – and that like Paul, <u>our highest and greatest obsession should be to know Christ</u>.

Let's string together the superlatives that Paul employed to describe Christ and his love and power – "incomparable, fullness, unsearchable, glorious, wide/long/high/deep, surpassing and immeasurable".

In my experience we have packaged up Christ without very much of the scale of him in place, and I have found that this scaled-down version of Christ had left me with a relatively meager form of Christianity.

There has got to be another way, a way that grasps the vast spectacle of Christ that Paul attempted to convey. It's as if Paul lifted up the edge of the covering that religion has placed over Christ, and allowed us to peep-in – and that glimpse is enough for us to abandon ourselves to his quest, 'to know Christ'.

Chapter 4
Lost For Words

I have often wondered why Paul *(in Romans 13 and 1 Corinthians 7)* seemed to believe that the return of the Lord was imminent, yet 2000 years later we are still waiting. It is as if Paul had such a clear view of the stunning accomplishments of the blood of Christ that he just naturally assumed Christ's return was almost upon them.

> ***It is this presumption of 'the magnificence that is found in Christ', which we must re-discover.***

But how far do we go?

Are there limits?

When Paul speaks of the immeasurable and unsearchable riches of Christ, he adds no caution that we should be careful not to step over the line - so the question for us is this; *"how far dare we go?"*

Let's say that our starting point is that 'Christ came to pay the penalty for our sins' – it is the universally accepted base-line that defines us. Christ came to earth and suffered and died so that we can put our faith in him and receive eternal life. John 3:16 and many scriptures like it support that this is true; "For God so loved the world that he gave his only Son, that whoever believes in him shall not perish but have eternal life".

Any belief less than this simple statement of faith would mean that we see Jesus as one of many pathways to God, or that we see him as a great example to us – *but such thinking is really no more than a broad philosophy, rather than a personal belief.*

If we believe that Jesus is merely one of many pathways to God, then we discredit his statement that "no one comes to the Father but by me" – we can't cherry-pick the bits of Christianity that suit us, so it can't really be called faith in Christ, if we do.

Now let's get back to our starting point. 'Christ came to save us from our sins' – he came as the substitute in our place and took the punishment that was due to us, upon himself. Over a lifetime we have clocked-up a significant number of sinful thoughts, words and deeds, not to mention the things we omitted to do *(that we should have done)*. It was like a load of unrighteousness that we carried around with us that obstructed our access to the Holy God - and Jesus took that load, suffered its punishment, and returned us to God.

Having grown up in a Christian home I always knew that Christ had died for my sins – I appreciated it and valued it, but it didn't make my heart race every time I thought about it. I just accepted that I was fortunate to grow up in a Christian home, and know about Jesus, and have my sins forgiven.

The reality was that it was all a little bit mundane.

We certainly didn't talk about it every day when I was growing up, nor did we go around with big smiles on our faces because we had been saved by Jesus – we just lived our lives, and went about the routines of work, and school, and family, and church.

We prayed. We talked to God about things; we recited the Lord's Prayer and the Apostles Creed at church, and said grace at mealtime. When we were little we also prayed our childhood prayers before bed, and if we had any troubles or needs we asked God to help. We did it because that's what Christians did, it was an established part of it all – *we did the same as everyone.*

Looking back now it was a bit odd in some ways, we had participated in the greatest act of love to ever occur in human history – *and we hardly gave much thought to what we had.*

Don't get me wrong, it's not that I was lacking in the emotional department – I could scream out in support of my football team as much as the next person. I knew how to love, and I knew how to feel deeply, but being a Christian didn't seem to require either of those things from me – it was a bit like being Australian (there are occasional moments of patriotism), but by-and-large my Christianity happened without much fan-fare.

As I grew through my adult years I added a lot of sophisticated Christian language and knowledge, but it didn't amount to any real change deep down. Even though I was as fully engaged as the next person, my Christianity remained much like my interest in football; there was no noticeable increase in 'the immeasurable and unsearchable riches of Christ' that Paul spoke of.

This went on until I was in my mid-fifties, the status quo was only tested when the Global Financial Crisis unraveled my business in property development – *it was time to re-appraise the whole Christian thing.*

There is a saying; *'The door that you go out of is the door that you come back in'.* It implies that life is progressive, and that we do not return to the bottom rung each time we re-enter the particular thing we are involved in – *(we step back on, at the level that we last stepped off).* For example; a thief may begin his career shoplifting, but once he has advanced to robbing banks he is unlikely to re-enter each new foray into thievery as a shoplifter, he will go straight back to where he left off, and rob another bank (he will re-enter the last door he came out of).

It happens in just about every field of human endeavor. Take falling-in-love for instance; it may begin with a casual glance across a crowded room, and then a shy conversation, holding hands may follow, and even perhaps some kissing – but there is no way the besotted couple will settle for the occasional casual glance after they have tried kissing.

For most of my life I thought that a 'casual glance' type of Christianity was all Christ had to offer me, it wasn't that I didn't want more, I just didn't know how to get there. It didn't matter how much of the language and rhetoric of Christianity I picked up along the way... I was stuck at first base.

I had spent the better part of my life coming and going from the same door – the door labeled "Jesus died for my sins". It wasn't until I had my personal world destabilized during the GFC that I began to examine the possibility that there were more doors. Doors that were beyond the one I had been using for years, doors that exposed me to more of the immeasurable and unsearchable riches of Christ.

Guess what?

I found more doors!

Chapter 5
New Doors

These new doors are actually revelations. They are the Holy Spirit revealing more and more of Christ.

They are different to the vast accumulation of Christian information that we amass just by our involvement in the huge culture of Christianity. They are not the latest teaching going around, or the new thing that 'God is doing' in one place or another – on the contrary they are old information because the Holy Spirit only reveals the testimony of Jesus, just as he has been doing for centuries.

Yet this old information is so transforming that it seems brand new – it's like we have been born again, *(again)* – only this time it really does make our hearts race, and we do seem to have a strange grin that we can't wipe off our face.

The first new revelation that I grasped was that "God is good".

It wasn't new information – *but it was new revelation.*

I had known that 'God was good' since I was a kid, but that knowledge was so mixed-in with the clutter of other Christian information that it had lost its real meaning. God was many things; Father, Holy, Lord, Judge, and more – each of these aspects of God's character elicited a different response in me with the result that God's goodness became a bit fuzzy and unpredictable.

I knew the scripture in Psalm 34:8 "taste and see that the Lord is good" – but it seemed equally likely that I might 'taste and see that the Lord is Judge', or 'taste and see that the Lord is angry at sin', or perhaps 'taste and see that the Lord has run out of patience with you - *and is disciplining you'*.

A lot of things had crept into my Christian Information Bank that were either influenced by the Old Covenant *(which Christ scrapped)*, or my own reasoning - which was based on my observations of the natural realm / rather than the spiritual realm *(which was my true home through Christ)*.

I had to sort them out – and conduct a thorough spring cleaning.

I had to throw out things that were a hang-over from Old Covenant religion / or had fallen in to my possession inadvertently by my involvement the 'culture of Christianity' *(as opposed to the person of Christianity)*.

I knew deep down that God was indeed good – I just needed to rid myself of the clutter in my mind that competed with his goodness.

We pick-up a lot of stuff along the way, "Everything happens for a reason" is one. The thought behind this is that God is orchestrating our circumstances to shape us in to vessels of usefulness. In other words God sends us tests, challenges and difficulties as a refining process – so that through these we will gradually be conformed into the image of Christ. You could say that God sends us bad stuff to make us into good people.

It didn't fit! There had to be another explanation.

Was God really in the business of sending people disabled babies, or untimely deaths, or any of the hardships that beset humanity – *and that there is some noble point to it all?*

Added to that there were other imponderables that we Christians had somehow rationalized away like; "If God is all-powerful and all-loving, why does he allow wars and famine and abuse?" I had to admit that this was a curly one – we Christians seemed to have dodged this by saying that sin was the root problem, but I found myself becoming less and less comfortable with these long-held responses. We seemed to be too eager to get God off the hook – instead of squaring-up to the real issue "Is God actually good?"

Then there was the old line that is often repeated at times of trouble "Don't worry, God is in control". But is he in control? Is he really in control when a plague strikes an African nation, or when a whole family dies in a freak car accident?

I didn't want to throw the baby out with the bath water, but neither did I want to continue using a bath full of water that was beyond its usefulness. I was beginning to think we had constructed a whole lot of our Christian thinking, on wrong information.

In the end I had to think again about the work that God had employed to repair the ills of humanity. There seemed to be two options:

1. Jesus came 2000 years ago and re-set human history back to its original design when he nailed the foolish experiment of Adam to his cross, and crucified it within his own death. We then receive the benefits of this fact simply by believing it to be true. Jesus completed our salvation in one fell-swoop and we partake of it all today, by believing he could be so good.

2. Jesus came 2000 years ago and repaired the breach between us and God by paying the penalty due to us. Now God engages with us (and all humanity) through our circumstances, and our resulting prayers and petitions. Jesus completed our salvation / but God controls the flow of its benefits according to our lifestyle, his choice, and his on-going shaping of our lives.

It was a question of whether Christ had actually completed the entire re-construction process 2000 years ago / or whether Christ got the thing started, and his Father was administering it to us *one teaspoon at a time* as he saw fit.

The more I looked at it, the more this teaspoon administration of Christ's work seemed out of place. 2 Peter 1:3 says "His divine power <u>has</u> given us everything we need for life and godliness" – I decided it was time to start believing this as a past tense fact.

Having crossed that line, all of the questions about God's involvement (or lack of it) in the circumstances of humanity where resolved. God didn't allow wars, famine and trouble – man did. God gave the whole created world to man - complete with full access to God's own divine life to maintain it. But Adam said to God "I will take it from here, it's mine and I will use it, and shape it, as I see fit".

In the fullness of time Jesus stepped into the human arena to bring restoration. He didn't fix the problems of the world because they weren't his to fix, but he gave humanity a way back to the original design – now man had full and free access to the divine life and godliness, that Adam abandoned. All the ills of humanity where swallowed up in the death and resurrection of Christ, the goodness of God was once again freely available to the world – through 'Christ in us'.

Of the two options open to me, I chose option 1.

God is indeed good, and he has made a way for this goodness to reach the people he loves (in spite of themselves). <u>God doesn't fix circumstances, he fixes people</u> – and our circumstances are in-turn fixed as we place our faith in the goodness of God, expressed so completely at the cross.

I had arrived at a new door – Jesus had paid the price of all the sin of my life, and now the goodness of God was my permanent companion simply by fixing my eyes on him – *(instead of the contrary message reported to me by the world and the religious system).*

How liberating is the revelation that God's goodness is always with me. It can't be diminished by any circumstance of life, or even my own failure to measure up.

The 'goodness of God' is very determined to reach me – *and I finally let it.*

Chapter 6
Letting God Love Me

It's no secret that 'God is love'.

What is a little less certain is 'The nature of that love'?

For the better part of my life I thought that God loved me because of 'who I am', now I realize he loves me because of 'who he is'. What I mean is that I thought the display of God's love into my life, was directly proportional to the God-pleasing lifestyle I was leading.

I knew that God expressed his eternal love for me by sending Christ to die for me (while I was yet a sinner, Romans 5:8) – but subsequent to this God-motivated event, I thought God's love couldn't reach me unless I was leading a life that measured-up to the gift of salvation.

Now I know the whole thing is God-motivated.

> **He loved me before I was saved (because of who he is),**
> **and he loves me just the same now**
> **– whether I am leading a life that reflects his love / or not.**

Let me explain this a bit further:

There is nothing I need to do to attract the full expression of God's love into my life, because it is not affected by what I do – *but what I believe*. Admittedly, I am very likely to lead a God-honoring life as a result of his love for me, but such a life is the overflow of God's love – not the means of receiving it.

This understanding enables me to live boldly and confidently as a Christian, no longer do I examine my lifestyle as the measure of receiving God's love – now I simply examine the power of the blood of Christ. This is the 'rest' that is referred to in many of Paul's letters, we cease from our labors in the sense that they do not qualify us for the flow of God's love and life into us. This 'resting' in the work of Christ, then motivates us to do great works of the Spirit.

I am no longer consumed with shame for past failings, or regret for human weaknesses that have marked my life – I swing my gaze across to Christ and live boldly as 'one made clean by his blood'. I refuse to allow my behavior (past/present/future) to define me... *(or my capacity to be the object of God's love).*

There is no 'me' apart from the perfection of Christ,
it is how the Father sees me.
And now I also see myself that way
- to do any less is to diminish the work of Christ.

The up-shot of removing my lifestyle from the equation, is that I can now lock-on to the work of Christ. All doubts about my qualification to partake in the inheritance I received from Christ are resolved; my performance is sidelined as a relevant factor in the outcomes I seek, as I day-by-day grow in my understanding of the nature of God's love.

The challenge for me is to believe that he is 'that good' – and that the salvation he provided is bigger than the frailties of my human condition.

Slowly, over time, I am learning to let myself be loved by God. He loves me for reasons I find difficult to comprehend, my natural inclination is to expect a love that is conditional on my performance – I am learning to see myself with the 'mind of Christ' *(I am slowly agreeing with God and his perspective)*, and this new reality is empowering me in ways that I never before dreamed possible.

Have you ever heard the saying "there is no such thing as a free lunch"? The suggestion is that everything comes with a price tag – even those things that

Chapter 6. Letting God Love Me

appear to be acts of generosity require a favor in return at some point in time.

God is not setting us up so that he can call in a favor later, we can take the free gift of God and do nothing with it if we like - it is up to us.

He is not purpose focused / he is people focused.

God is not keeping score, nor is he waiting for the right moment to lean on us – he has set us free, completely free. He has given us the gift of life, and has absolutely no expectation in return – and now as far as he is concerned, his only desire is that we receive the gift.

That is freedom!

That is love... God's way.

It is a love that is so unconditional that a surprising thing results – we find ourselves surrendering to the wonder of it, much like Jesus did in the book of John 5:20 "For the Father loves the Son and shows him all he does." It is a love that brings out the best in us – *Christ himself loving through us.*

This love gives us a second chance, not because is carries with it a high expectation – but because it carries no expectation. In the place of expectation it offers 'the adventure of life in the Spirit' – *for free*. This 'life in the Spirit' has contained within it an energizing effect – instead of producing good works through religious expectation, it produces 'works of life' through the indwelling Christ.

It is a way to live that religion couldn't provide.

This new way to live can only spring forth from us when it is unfettered by the old way of religious obligation.

Over the years I have heard many statements that attempt to constrain Christians within a life of religious obligation. The statements that follow seem to have a ring of truth to them, but in the end they are nothing more that well-crafted legalism disguised as grace.

'God could have taken us home to heaven the minute we were saved, but he left us on earth to do our part in the great commission'.

'Our existence within the church is a purpose driven one – we were created for the job that God fitted to our personality and gifting'.

These, and many statements like them, have a lack of trust at their core – they don't trust the Holy Spirit to craft our lives into a thing of beauty and meaning. They constrain the human spirit in a way it was never designed for – and use the means of religion, obligation, guilt and ambition as tools to achieve their goal.

But they make a mockery of the human spirit – because we weren't designed to be constrained, we were designed to be free.

We were designed to be so consumed by the love of God that a spontaneous life of 'goodness and mercy' overflowed from us. John 4:14 says "Instead, the water that I will give to him will become in him a spring of water, welling up into eternal life" – *this is the way we were originally designed, and subsequently re-made by the blood of Christ.*

The biggest inhibitor to this life is our doubt that such a life is possible.

It is a door that lays open before us all, but our insecurities hold us back. We are so used to living a life that is bound by the rules of 'sowing and reaping' that we can spend years, and even decades, on the wrong side of this 'door to life'.

We circle in and out of the door 'Christ died for my sins' - when in reality, this first door has opened the way for us into another door, *which is actually the overflow of that event.*

This new door of 'God's love' is both immeasurable and unsearchable – yet is has a mechanism within it that keeps the majority of Christians out. We cannot pass through it while carrying the baggage of self-effort. This door strips us bare; to pass through it we must be clothed only in the love of God which is ours in Christ.

We bring no human quality or response; we simply let God love us because of who he is.

Chapter 6. Letting God Love Me

It is the great dare of faith.

'Dare we believe that God's love is bigger than our long-held limitations, and dare we let go of our insecurities and walk through that door, with nothing as our covering but Christ himself'.

Chapter 7
Trusting in His Word

It is absolutely essential that we pass through the doors labeled 'God is good' and 'God loves me' before attempting to base our lives on his word. If we have not resolved these two fundamentals as *'having been fully satisfied by Christ'*, then everything we read in God's word will be conditional on some human response or virtue.

God does not require that we bring any personal qualification to attend his great banquet; he simply beckons us to come from the highways and byways of life – and clothe ourselves in the righteousness of Christ, see Luke 14:23.

Once we have laid hold of the fact that Christ alone qualifies us to partake in the goodness and love of God, we are ready to discover the 'words of life' contained in the bible.

In effect, the blood of Christ qualifies us *as if* we were 'Christ himself' dining at his Father's banquet. We have been so hidden in the work of Christ that there is not even a sideways glance from the Father as we take our place of honor. When the Father looks upon us he sees the perfection of Christ (which is our new nature). We can only be disqualified if we attempt to wear a garment made from our own virtue. To do so would be an offence to our host, it would be akin to wearing the filth of fallen humanity to the great wedding banquet of Christ – such is the meager worth of our own virtue, when compared to the stunning glory of the righteousness given to us by Christ.

The Surpassing Greatness Of Christ

We must bring this same bold certainty to the word of God.

As we do so it will appear that we have a brand new bible. This new bible will contain hope and life and promises which had previously seemed like a list of religious hurdles God required us to jump – it will seem like the word of God has been re-written just for us.

Simple scriptures like Hebrews 13:5 "Never will I leave you; never will I forsake" will take on new meaning – they will become our personal assurance that God's presence is continually ours because of Christ, and not measured-out to us, according to our personal goodness.

Others like Colossians 3:3 "For you died, and your life is now hidden with Christ in God" will take on new meaning as we learn to rest in the sufficiency of Christ.

Perhaps you have never taken literally a scripture like 2 Peter 1:3 "By his divine power he has given us everything we need for life and godliness." And verse 4 "Through these he has given us his very great and precious promises, so that through them you may participate in the divine nature".

**All of these scriptures are qualified for us by the blood of Christ, there is nothing we need do to make them so
- <u>but simply believe that they are so.</u>**

Every believer has latent within them every promise contained in God's word. To actively participate in these promises we simply believe that Christ's blood has qualified us, and then we rest in the certainty of his sacrifice instead of our own attempts to be religious or righteous.

Religion taught us that there were certain practices and methods that activated the word of God. These practices ranged from loud prayer, continuous prayer, group prayer, intense worship, unity in the body of Christ, unbroken prayer circles, strict observance of quiet times, systematic reading of the bible, etc. etc.

In reality these methods and systems attempted to create something that was

Chapter 7. Trusting in His Word

in us all along, they caused us to believe in 'what we do' instead of 'what Christ has done'. Romans 10:8 says "The word of God is near you, in your mouth and in your heart" – we don't need to drum-up God's approval by some demonstrative, intense or desperate activity – we need to simply rest in the reality of the life of God's word which is now within us, *as our new nature.*

One small child, who looks into the eyes of Jesus and believes - has as much power as a thousand prayer warriors who are storming heaven with loud and frenzied prayer. *God always responds to the sacrifice of Christ and never to the intensity of people*. It doesn't matter how much we believe God should respond to us because of our religious fervor, he will not re-make the gospel of Christ just to satisfy our insecure hearts.

We can, and must, stand on God's word without depending on the trigger of any human action.

**The bible is the written word, and Jesus is the Living Word,
we must always remember that our confidence in the Living Word
- is the thing that activates the promises in the written word.**

With that in mind our objective in reading the bible should always be to discover Christ. If we read the bible to find a formula for solving life's problems or to uncover a form of lifestyle that we believe will please God – then we have missed the whole point.

Towards the end of the book of John in chapter 20 verse 31 the real objective of the written word is clearly articulated. "But these things are written that you may believe that Jesus is the Christ, the Son of God, and that by believing you may <u>have life</u> in his name". We read the word to discover Jesus, and as we believe in him we receive life. This is the primary purpose of the written word.

The Holy Spirit has a similar mandate to the written word. In John 15:26 we read "When the Counselor comes, whom I will send to you from the Father, the Spirit of truth who goes out from the Father, he will testify about me". The Holy Spirit testifies or reveals Jesus to us – it is his primary purpose.

The Word and the Spirit agree – they reveal Jesus in perfect harmony.

The reason they are both focused on revealing Jesus is that without a revelation of Jesus the bible is a legalistic document (it tells us the rules for living), but with the revelation of Jesus it becomes a life-giving document – John 10:10 "He came that we might <u>have life</u> and have it abundantly".

The bible may be many different things to many different people; it contains great history, poetry, wisdom, and insight into responsible living – and all of these things can be obtained in some degree by reading it. But it wasn't given to us for any of those reasons – it was intended to reveal Jesus to us, so that we might believe in him, and have life.

Not that we might learn about how Jesus lived and copy the example of his lifestyle – but that we might realize that there is a completely different way to live that is so superior to mere discipleship as to render it trite, it is that we might grasp son-ship and allow Christ to actually live in us, and through us.

The disciples became apostles when Jesus went to the Father and sent them the Spirit in his place. And similarly we must progress from servitude to son-ship.

This is the great surprise of the word, as we cease our search for the things that might qualify us in God's eyes, and fix our eyes on the one who does qualify us – we begin to discover the divine flow of life that he came to give us. It was there all along, but our obsession with 'doing the right thing' obscured the gospel from our view - *'Jesus did the right thing for us.'*

This can take some adjusting to. It can seem irresponsible and self-absorbed to deliberately disconnect our focus from 'our response' to God – and fix it on 'receiving life' from Jesus. Yet it is the reason he came, 'He came to give us life' – *and it is not for us to tell Jesus how he should go about crafting our salvation.*

We do the high price that he paid for our salvation, a great dis-service, when we insist on a life of mere religious servitude. He died to make us sons and daughters of the Most High God, anything less diminishes the value of his blood – *he came to give us life, not to perpetuate the deeds of Adam.*

So my request to you is this; take a leap as you have possibly never done before.

Chapter 7. Trusting in His Word

Leap out of the security of trying to please God, and land in Jesus *(who is God's pleasure in us)*. It may defy every religious bone in your body – but do it anyway, dare to believe that he loves you enough to save you in spite of yourself. Dare to imagine that he crafted a salvation so extravagant and lavish, that your only part is to come to him – and have life.

This 'life' that is associated with Jesus is quite different to our normal understanding of 'life'. I had always understood this 'life' to be specifically related to our earthly circumstances – as if the life that Jesus came to give me was an improved version of the one I was already living – *but one that had fewer problems and difficulties*. I know now that the life Jesus came to give me is quite separate from the comings and goings of my existence in the natural realm; it is a 'life' that comes from being re-connected to his Father. It has spin-offs into the natural realm, but it is primarily about something far superior to what we see and experience here – *it is that we have been re-born with the nature of God as eternal divine-natured beings.*

Most Christians I know would gladly settle for a 'life' that repairs and restores their earthly issues and concerns. The life that we lead in the natural realm demands attention and we are easily pulled towards the demands it makes. It can take some very deliberate effort to step back from the daily concerns of life on earth, and direct our attention to a realm that we can't see or experience in the same way.

Yet that is where the 'life' that Jesus offers us originates from. So we must tear our focus away from the demands of planet earth and fix it firmly on Christ, and having done so the concerns of this realm will participate in the overflow of his life in us too.

This is where the word of God finally began to make sense to me. I had been attempting to drag it into my circumstances in the form of promises, methods and lifestyle – but Christ had already taken me out of the location of these circumstances and translated me to heaven. I needed to re-calibrate my understanding of the personal earth-based issues of my life, and see them from the perspective of my new eternal home.

I had been reading the word of God to find solutions to my earth-based problems and needs, but I finally understood that the 'life' that Jesus came to give me was not primarily concerned with those earth-based issues; the resolution of these issues (of the natural realm) was merely the secondary outcome of my salvation, and they were resolved as the 'overflow' of his primary purpose.

In fact, the entire workings of my Christian faith had been wrapped up in the secondary issues – my faith had been essentially about my relationship to the natural environment of my life - *my work, my relationships, my church activities*. Yet the 'life' that Jesus gave me was spiritual life, and it was about a realm much higher than the natural realm.

I'm not suggesting that the natural realm is not relevant or important, but rather that everything that takes place here should be the overflow of the primary truth of our salvation *(that we have received Christ's life)*. In fact my fixation with the secondary issues had seriously limited God's hand upon them, <u>because they could *only* be resolved as an overflow of the primary fact of Christ's life in me</u>.

If I wanted the overflow... *then I needed to go higher first*.

In short, I needed to stop trying to find ways to get God to fix my earthly problems, and rest in the *crazy notion* that my real problem was not of this earth – it was an eternal problem, and it was fixed when Jesus gave me his life. When I made this discovery my earth-based problems gradually fell in to line with the amazing truth of the finished work of Christ – *you could say 'they began to align themselves with a higher truth'.*

This is why Jesus went around teaching about 'the kingdom of God' – because once we understand our true home, the issues of our temporary home come into order.

I said all of that to say this;
**the life that Jesus gave has translated us to a new kingdom
– and now we must approach the bible as citizens of that kingdom.**

Chapter 7. Trusting in His Word

The bible is no longer a list of principles for right living, or useful tips for navigating our way through the obstacle course of life – it is the unfolding revelation of our new eternal nature, our guidebook for discovering how to walk in the Spirit.

Citizens of the kingdom of God, and citizens of planet earth, read the bible in opposing ways. The difference is how they perceive righteousness. Citizens of the kingdom of God have grasped that their righteousness is a fully paid-for gift from Christ; they do not need to look to the bible to find tips to shore-up their confidence to stand in the presence of God. Citizens of planet earth see their righteousness as a combination of the work of the cross and their own lifestyle; consequently they read the bible to discover their part in maintaining their standing before the presence of God.

This new way of reading God's word has been the third new door that I have passed through. I will never again read the bible as one who is 'a work in progress', I will always enter the door of God's word as one made completely righteous by the blood of Christ.

I have welded the old door shut – my only way into the word of God from now on, is as one who is a fully fledged citizen of heaven. This citizenship automatically became mine when I received the 'life' of Christ – this life is my new nature *(Christ came to give it to me – and I have taken possession of it)*.

By placing my confidence in the *'righteousness-giving life'* I received from Christ, I now read the written word as one who is hidden in 'the living word' himself. He lives in me, and the word of God now pertains to me in exactly the same way that it pertains to Christ himself.

Chapter 8
The Living Word – In Me

The further I progress through these new doors of my understanding – the more they are at odds with the observations of my natural eyes.

The notion that Jesus 'lives in me' has no counterpart in the realm of normal human understanding. It is important therefore, that we do not fall into the trap of relegating it to terms that we are more familiar with.

'Jesus lives in me' is not a matter of his mission, his example, or even his memory living in us. It is neither figurative nor philosophical – it is simply a literal fact. Jesus has made his home in my spirit – I am now the permanent habitation of the Son of the Living God.

There have been many great people in history who have left behind a remarkable legacy of service. After they die it is often the case that others pick-up the baton passed on by the original person, and carry on their legacy - in some respects the first person 'lives-on' in those that follow.

This is not the way that Jesus lives in us.

Jesus moved-into us by crucifying our old nature, and in its place he filled us with his own nature. Don't misunderstand the word 'nature'; it is not the same as we might use the word to describe a naughty child. Jesus didn't just deal with our naughty side, so that our nice side could come to the surface. If that were the case then Jesus would pal-up to us when we are being nice, and shy away when we are not.

The presence of Jesus within us goes much deeper than our good behavior (or the lack of it); it is a total transformation of the spiritual substance that we are made of - Jesus crucified our dead-to-God spirit, and he re-birthed us with the Spirit of God.

Back in chapter four I asked the question; *"But how far do we go? Are there limits?"*

It is important to bring an adventurous spirit with us as we attempt to grasp the scale of the salvation Christ gave us. We want to lay hold of our full inheritance, not simply a neatly packaged version that the Old Nature finds palatable.

I have made the point a number of times that we *'do Christ no service'* when we understate or underestimate the accomplishments of his shed blood. He suffered terribly for us that we might walk fully in the 'life' he came to give; we value this sacrifice most - when we abandon ourselves to it completely.

There was a time when I thought those who claimed to be 'living by faith' were religious extremists who lived on the fringes of Christianity. They were dropouts who used Christianity as an excuse to be irresponsible and lazy – they seemed to have no grasp of the 'real world' and had opted for nothing more than social-welfare dressed-up as spirituality. *And besides; it didn't seemed to be working for them very well.*

However Paul says in 2 Corinthians 5:7 "For we live by faith, not by sight".

It didn't appear that Paul was putting 'living by faith' out there as an option we could choose / or not. Rather he seemed to be saying that it was part of the package deal that came with faith in Christ. In fact, (to take it a step further) he seemed to be suggesting that we would be mad not to live by faith. Given the spectacular life-flow that Christ came to give us, why would we even contemplate not surrendering ourselves to its ability to carry us through everything.

That's the point; we don't instinctively cast ourselves fully into the safe-keeping of Christ, because we don't see that such an option is realistically open to us. Instead we choose a hybrid of our own design, and construct our sense of security from our management of the 'good and evil' equation.

If we could truly see the immeasurable and unsearchable substance of 'Christ in me' then we would completely entrust ourselves to him in a heartbeat - <u>but we don't trust what we can't see,</u> so our Christianity is more defined by the culture and the clichés, than by our bold trust in Jesus himself.

It is imperative that we break through this log-jamb. We were designed to be carried aloft by the breath of God – *(it is not an optional extra... which is only taken up by the super-spiritual).*

We only break through as we believe a truth which initially has no physical evidence to support it *(but the written word of God)* – 'Christ has made his home in me'. As we begin to place our confidence in the claims of the written word, the Living Word begins to impact our physical world, and the evidence follows.

> ***The written word reveals the Living Word***
> ***- we believe it,***
> ***and then the Living Word takes over***
> ***and we are transformed by his indwelling presence.***

At that point we cease to be adherents to a belief system, or participants in the activities of an organization – we have become the literal dwelling place of the Spirit of The Living God. As a result, our life ceases to be defined by our lifestyle and religious activities, but is defined entirely by our faith in the in-dwelling presence of God.

Chapter 9
A Deeper Look

Up to this point we have progressed through a series of doors:

- Christ died for my sins.
- God is good.
- God loves me.
- I can trust in his word.
- The Living Word lives in me.

It's time now to use these foundational truths as a launching pad into 'Life in the Spirit'.

In 1990 the Hubble telescope was launched into space to get a better view of the cosmos. From its orbit above the earth it could see previously unknown stars and galaxies without the interference generated by the earth's hazy atmosphere.

These galaxies each contained hundreds of billions of stars *(stars just like our own Sun)*, and the Hubble telescope scanned the sky recording the vast array on view – upwards of 100 billion galaxies, each containing hundreds of billions of stars, not to mention planets and moons.

The Surpassing Greatness Of Christ

In September 2003 the operators of Hubble decided to undertake a short term experiment, they would concentrate their view on a very small part of the sky that contained no visible stars or galaxies. They decided to view a spot in the sky equivalent to a 1mm x 1mm square held 1m away – *not a very big area at all*. They would lock-on to that empty spot for 10 continuous days to see if there was anything there that was generating light. This experiment has become known as 'Hubble Deep Field'.

At the end of that 10 day period they were stunned by what was revealed – this small speck in the sky contained 10,000 previously undiscovered galaxies (each containing 100 billion+ stars).

This discovery caused scientists all over the world to re-think the scale of the universe – the whole thing was staggeringly bigger than they had ever imagined before.

The scale of the universe and the scale of our salvation have similarities; there is more to Christ than meets the eye. Paul puts the 'immeasurable and unsearchable' nature of Christ out there, to draw us in to the adventure of discovering him. I can almost hear him saying "this salvation is bigger than you think" – get a view of the scale of the thing that you are in, and it will totally blow your mind.

For the most part of my life, my view of Christianity was akin to looking at the night sky from my back verandah – *it was spectacular, but also limited*. 'Christ died for my sins' was all I could see.

The new doors I listed at the start of this chapter are like a view from the Hubble telescope, they have outlined a larger vista of Christ. They have opened me up to more; they have called forth the adventurer in me, and set me on a course for a 'Deep Field' exploration.

In the epistle of John chapter 3, Jesus has a visit from a leading Pharisee named Nicodemus – Jesus explains to Nicodemus about being 'born again'. He puts to Nicodemus a concept that was previously unknown to the Jews, and it blows away all of Nicodemus previously neatly-packaged theology. But that wasn't the end of it, in verse 12 Jesus says this; "I have spoken to you of earthly things and you do not believe; how then will you believe if I speak to you of heavenly things?"

Jesus seems to be saying; "to be 'Born Again' is the tip of the iceberg (it is the starting point) - the view of Christianity from your back verandah". But there is more, I can also show you heavenly things, it would be a truly 'Deep Field' view of your salvation, that exposes you to wonders beyond your wildest imagination.

It's the same sentiment that is expressed in Paul's letter to the Ephesians 1:18; "I pray that the eyes of your heart may be enlightened in order that you may know the hope to which he has called you, the riches of his glorious inheritance in the saints, and his incomparably great power for us who believe". Paul prays that the Ephesians would get a Deep Field view - *a view of reality as God sees it.*

For years my ability to walk in the spirit was limited to the scale of my view of salvation. It wasn't enough to have a 'back verandah' view of Christ – I needed to discover the deeper outcomes of his work on the cross, so that I could boldly step into the new identity he had provided for me. The more I could see the scale of the thing Jesus had done, the more I could walk boldly in the power of the Spirit.

The heavenly things that Jesus spoke of are the real game-changer for Christians. They expose us to the staggering potential within each of us, because Christ has done so much more than we knew.

In Hebrews chapter 6 we read these words; "Therefore let us leave the elementary teachings about Christ and go on to maturity, not laying again the foundation of repentance from acts that lead to death, and of faith in God, instructions about baptisms, the laying on of hands, the resurrection of the dead, and eternal judgment". These are the elementary teachings of Christianity, they are the view from the back verandah – yet for much of my life they were the door that I came and went from, they were the sum of my Christianity.

The Surpassing Greatness Of Christ

In the following chapters we will look at Christ, his work on the cross, and our resultant inheritance in a deeper way. We will position ourselves above the atmosphere of the elementary teachings and focus our gaze on the riches of his glorious inheritance in the saints, and his incomparably great power for us who believe.

The 'Kingdom of God' has more doors that await our discovery.

Chapter 10
The Kingdom of God

Have you ever wondered why Jesus continually taught about 'The Kingdom of God', yet in Luke 8:10 He said; The knowledge of the secrets of the kingdom of God has been given to you *(the disciples),* but to others I speak in parables, so that, 'though seeing, they may not see; though hearing, they may not understand.'?

What was it that enabled the disciples to understand things that others couldn't?

Could it be that the disciples had a unique capacity to understand 'The Kingdom of God' because they lived every day in Jesus presence - *who was the living expression of it.* Others who did not have the continual presence of Jesus were less likely to 'get it' – they heard his teaching and saw his miracles, but didn't recognize the kingdom from which these came. In John 6:26 Jesus says; "I tell you the truth, you want to be with me because I fed you, not because you understood the miraculous signs".

It is imperative that we progress beyond the crowd in Luke 8:10 who, 'though seeing - do not see; though hearing - do not understand.'

To do that we must venture beyond the constraints of a form of Christianity that is stuck in the issues of life on earth, we must gain a view of Christ's work from a vantage point above the hazy atmosphere of all that clamors for our attention here – and adjust our focus onto 'Christ alone', to see the deeper substance of our salvation.

It is interesting that the scripture above in Luke 8:10 is also recorded in Matthew 13:11 and Mark 4:11 but there is no reference to it in the gospel of John. Further to this, the first three gospels contain many records of the parables of Jesus, but the gospel of John contains none.

In my opinion, the book of John exposes to us, that which the parables in Matthew, Mark and Luke concealed. John has laid out for us the workings of the kingdom of God, without the hidden meaning contained in the parables. The first three gospels are more of a 'back verandah' view of Jesus, the gospel of John positions us for a deeper view of the amazing salvation which is ours in Christ. There is nothing wrong with a 'back verandah' view, it was all I had for 55 years – but to see 'the riches of his glorious inheritance in the saints, and his incomparably great power for us who believe' is what we were born for.

The kingdom of God is the home that Jesus came to return us to. All believers will live there after they die. Some however, will bring the reality of that kingdom forward into their present day lives as they lay hold of the truth of it now. They will be like the disciples to whom 'The knowledge of the secrets of the kingdom of God had been given' – because they have seen who Jesus really is, in all his glory and majesty.

The gospel of John stands apart from the first three gospels. The gospels of Matthew, Mark and Luke are known as the synoptic gospels – which means they give a broad overview of the subject matter. This is clarified in Luke 1:3, in his own words Luke confirms that he has written 'an orderly account' of the things that had happened.

In contrast, John has a different objective as found in John 20:31 "These things are written that you may believe that Jesus is the Christ, the Son of God, and that by believing you may have life in his name". John's objective was to do more than provide an accurate record of Jesus life, it was to present a view of Jesus that would expose us to the spiritual realm from which Jesus lived his life – and as we believe this deeper information about Jesus, we can partake of the same life-source that he did.

If you have read the previous books in this trilogy you will be aware that my

Chapter 10. The Kingdom of God

worldly security was stripped away from me in the Global Financial Crisis about eight years ago. It was primarily the book of John that stopped me in my tracks at this time - as I attempted to discover a better way to understand my faith.

John presents concepts and revelations about Jesus that are like a view from above the clouds, <u>his gospel is written from the spiritual realm looking back to the physical realm</u>, whereas the other gospels are written from the physical realm looking up to the spiritual realm.

Ephesians 1:3 says; "God has blessed us in the <u>heavenly realms</u> with every spiritual blessing in Christ".

Ephesians 2:6 says; "And God raised us up with Christ and seated us with him in the <u>heavenly realms</u>".

It is the view of Jesus from the heavenly (or spiritual) realm that provides us with 'The knowledge of the secrets of the kingdom of God' – as we gain this view the secrets are unveiled to us. These secrets presented me with new doorways that I was previously unaware of, doorways that have changed my life forever.

Chapter 11
In The Beginning Was the Word

John jumps straight in, there is no preamble or introduction to get us ready for what would follow, he seems determined from the very start to get us thinking from a different perspective. John 1:1 "In the beginning was the Word".

John puts us off-balance from the outset so that we do not immediately think of Jesus as a man, it took John another 13 verses before he introduces the humanity of Jesus "The Word became flesh and dwelt among us".

Jesus is not primarily a human being.

Jesus existence before he clothed himself in human form was the real Jesus – and John calls that existence 'The Word'. Jesus existence without the covering of the flesh was no less real than his existence as a man, he existed as a spiritual being before he was a man / while he was a man / and when he left his humanity behind, and returned to his Father.

He was the 'Word' before he became a man, and also while he was a man. Even though Jesus entered into human form, it was not this 'human form' that defined his being; it was his union with his Father that defined him.

The body of flesh and blood that Jesus wore-around for about 33 years may well be the Jesus we relate to most, but it barely scratches the surface in regard to the true scale of his being.

Even though he humbled himself and became a man, he was more 'in his Father' - than he was 'in the flesh'.

John 1:4 "In him was life". Or as John puts it in his first letter, 1 John 1:1 "this we proclaim concerning the Word of life". *The Word had Life.* In John 5:26 we read "For as the Father has life in himself, so he has granted the Son to have life in himself".

He had the same life as the Father, divine eternal life – *even before he entered the flesh, and took on our physical kind of life.*

He was the Word that had Life.

And that Life was the Light of men, John 1:4… *the light of the world.*

All of this can seem a bit cryptic; it's not the way we normally talk. That's because John is describing the beginning, before there was a material creation – he is describing Jesus before he entered into physical form.

John is giving us a chance to perceive Jesus differently, before the story of his life and death color-in our thinking. And for very good reason; the Jesus who lives in us today is the same Jesus who existed before there was any material world. He is the real Jesus who doesn't need a human body to exist – because he is the great 'I am'.

This Jesus clothed himself in the flesh twice.

The first time was when he was born as a baby in Bethlehem.

The second time was when he was born into the hearts of people like you and me.

The very same Jesus who constrained himself into human likeness (Philippians 2:7) as a little baby boy, has declared in John 17:26 that 'he himself will be in us'. In this scripture Jesus makes a clear distinction between the love of God being *in us* – and he, <u>himself</u> being *in us*. In the first instance we are the objects of God's unconditional love, in the second instance we are the recipients of Jesus himself.

There is no more to 'the Jesus' that was born into a little baby in Bethlehem,

Chapter 11. In The Beginning Was the Word

than 'the Jesus' that is born into us, as we receive his life when we are born again. The full substance of Jesus Christ is as much in us today, as it was when he saved the world on the cross 2000 years ago.

That is the reason John calls Jesus 'The Word – that had Life – that was Light" and why Jesus calls himself 'The Way, the Truth, the Life, the Light of the World, the Gate, the Resurrection and the Life, the Root, the Vine, the Bright Morning Star, etc. etc. – *he is so very much bigger than his humanity!*

It's hard to avoid the obvious questions;

What does it mean to be the vessel that walks-around such a stunningly spiritual being 24/7?

How does it change things for us, to know that the one 'through whom all things were made' - has now made his home in us?

Are we content to carry on as we are, knowing that the Son of the Living God has planted himself into our hearts?

Jesus had done it once before with spectacular results – he had inhabited the flesh. Back then it was a man from Nazareth, *(a baby who grew up to be a man)* – **a man who somehow understood the union he had with his heavenly father...** ***in spite of all that 'being a human' threw at him.*** That first time was different - because the flesh part was in perfect agreement with the spirit part *(right from the word go)*. The whole person was instinctively tuned-in to the heart of God.

It was different after that first time. With each one that followed since, Jesus had to overcome the natural instincts of the flesh part - he had to slowly reveal to them who he was, by opening up the eyes of their heart. Once the eyes of their heart began to work, the instinct of knowing God's heart followed.

Some, like Paul, got the shock treatment – brilliant light, blindness, brokenness... *and the instinctive knowledge of God followed.*

But most he led gently to understand who he was, he quietly waited until they got to the end of themselves, so they could see passed all the flesh stuff - and realize that God lived in them. The same Spirit that lived in the Nazarene had also made his home in all those that the Nazarene had given his light to, with the expressed purpose that they be tuned-in to the heart of God.

This new doorway has been like a brilliant flash of understanding that has made everything else clear to me. It may not have been as outwardly dramatic as Paul's experience on the road to Damascus, but it has had the same illuminating effect. The reason Jesus has taken residence in my heart is so that I can instinctively know the heart of God – just like Jesus himself does.

John 17:6 says, "I have *revealed you*, to those whom you gave me out of the world" – it is what the 'Word' does... he declares and reveals the heart of God.

Chapter 12
How Far Do We Go?

I have asked the question 'How far do we go?' several time so far in this book.

We have a built-in reluctance to accept that our salvation can be dramatically more than we observe with our natural eyes. We observe our lives; our circumstances, our weaknesses, and our human condition in general – and relegate the 'presence of Jesus in us' to the metaphorical or figurative, rather than the practical and actual.

In other words; we look to the natural evidence
- to determine a spiritual reality.

For some, the journey of grasping the presence of 'Christ within' can seem like just another spiritual hurdle we must jump, it seems so far from our present-day reality that our shoulders slump at the thought of attaining something so lofty.

In reality this can be the shortest journey we ever make, it is a journey of the heart – not a journey of human effort or religious activity. If we so chose, the journey can happen in an instant.

Life is like that. We often adjust our view of reality when new information is presented to us. A woman who has difficulty conceiving may be convinced that she will never be a mother, but one day she falls pregnant, and this new information changes all of her previous notions. The new information can't be denied, there is a baby growing inside her – every thought must now be re-aligned to agree with this new reality.

The reality of Jesus inside us is no less real than a pregnancy; it's just that the pregnancy is a natural event, whereas the presence of Jesus is a spiritual event. We know that the pregnancy is true because of the physical evidence, and we know that Jesus lives in us because of the evidence of the word and the Spirit.

Our problem is that we are not accustomed to accepting the evidence of the word and the Spirit when making our life-size decisions. We want God to come up with evidence that convinces us through logical reasoning based on physical appearance, rather than through invisible truths that we accept by belief. We are like the disciple Thomas who said 'unless I can touch Jesus I won't believe he is alive', and he was castigated by Jesus for it. The Thomas approach is out of sync with the word and the Spirit, the way of the Spirit is that we believe first - and then the evidence follows in its own time.

Modern day Christianity is strong on the rhetoric and language of faith, but weak on the bare-faced belief. We are more likely to see a pleasing Christian lifestyle, than a person standing with an unshakable conviction in the blood of Christ.

And so Christianity has devolved into a culture that hopes God will come through, rather than an immovable confidence in his presence and power.

But it doesn't have to be that way; we can be profoundly tuned-in to the heart of God – all it takes is that we change our minds and begin believing the improbable notion that 'Jesus lives in me'.

> ***We must arrest our instinctive thought processes***
> ***– and agree with God.***

There is no middle ground here; it's not enough to dip our toe in the water – we must jump in the deep end.

In my case I jumped in the deep-end when all of the rhetoric of Christianity had failed me, I did it because the cross-road I faced was either; absolute confidence in God / or abandon my faith altogether. Inadvertently I found myself in the very place where God wanted me to be, he didn't want me to live in a luke-warm version of Christianity – he wanted me to be hot or cold... *and I chose hot.* Not 'hot' in regard to my religious fervor, but hot in regard to my unshakable conviction that God can be trusted.

Revelation 3:16 puts it very plainly; "So, because you are lukewarm, *neither hot* nor *cold,* I am about to spit you out of my mouth".

It is this 'wallowing in the shallows' kind of faith that obscured from view the thing I needed most, I wanted the outcomes of unshakable belief / to be produced by the luke-warm Thomas kind of faith. I wanted Jesus to re-make my salvation to suit my shallow confidence – and I only realized it when I came to the end of myself.

So the question remains 'How far do we go?'

The only possible answer can be *'we go all the way'.* To do otherwise would be to treat the blood of Christ as a convenient commodity, rather than the most precious possession of humanity. If we do not take a 'Deep Field' view of our salvation then we remain people who live a shallow faith that suits the insecurities of our flesh. We were not designed for such a life – we were designed to live as people so full of the life of Christ, that we barely resemble our previous condition.

The adventure of faith should be like the early settlers who pushed-in to new frontiers just because they were there, and because they wanted to have the best life possible. Each day was an opportunity to discover more new territory; they never looked back, always scanning the distant horizons to enter-in to the new wonders ahead.

Paul prays that we would grasp 'how high and long and wide and deep is the love of Christ' – I doubt that Christ will tell me "you went too far" when I see him face-to-face at the end of my life. More likely he would say "there was so much more, it was yours for the taking – all you had to do was believe I could give you so much".

The Surpassing Greatness Of Christ

One simple decision remains; 'will we be so bold as to believe that Christ has given us a salvation beyond our wildest dreams – and will we abandon our religious reservations and fears, and grasp hold of it'?

Chapter 13
I No Longer Live, But Christ Lives in Me

At first, the idea of 'Christ living in me' was too difficult for me to grab hold of. It was like ancient writings etched on the wall of a lost cave – the meaning was beyond me, I had no internal code for translating the truth of it. Yet somehow it resonated with me at the same time – *I knew instinctively that it was true, I just didn't understand how.*

The only faculty I could bring was human reasoning, *and it wasn't up to the task.*

In Colossians 1:26 & 27 Paul talks of a mystery that was hidden for ages but now revealed to us, "The mystery is Christ in you". I couldn't unlock the code of this mystery with my normal human faculties, I needed more – I needed a higher ability that would enable me to master the hidden meaning.

Paul speaks in Galatians 2:20 of a condition that we can easily limit to *Paul alone* because of his unique calling and experience – "I have been crucified with Christ, I no longer live but Christ lives in me". We think that Paul made this statement because he had given up everything for the 'cause of Christ'. Yet many other scriptures refer to the 'death' that was wrought in *us* as a result of our salvation, that have no connection to Paul's personal experience - Colossians 3:3 "For you died, and your life is now hidden with Christ in God".

Paul wasn't referring to a personal act of self-sacrifice; quite the contrary, he was referring to the sacrifice of Christ - and he personally joined himself to that sacrifice by placing faith in Jesus. Paul considers himself dead in so far as his dependence on human reasoning was concerned, and it was this that unlocked the hidden meaning for Paul. He could see something that was a mystery to the masses, because his human reasoning was removed from the process... *and replaced with the mind of Christ.*

And what is 'the mind of Christ?'

What exactly does Jesus know?

He 'knows his Father' - is what he knows!

This knowledge is not grounded in human reasoning – *it was revelation knowledge that his spirit knew.*

All through the book of John we read Jesus speaking of 'knowing his Father' – it is a reoccurring theme that we inadvertently read-over, but it is the hidden key to the powerful life Jesus led. Jesus had no power greater than we have, all he had was his knowledge of his Father – it was this knowledge that gave him the capacity and confidence to live a supernatural life.

This knowledge is not *knowing* everything about God (theology); rather it is to know and understand God's heart. It is a knowledge that is available to every believer, as Jesus points out in John 17:25-26 "Righteous Father, though the world does not know you, I know you, and they (the disciples) know that you sent me. **I have made you known to them**, and will continue to make you known in order that the love you have for me may be in them and that I myself may be in them".

Jesus is explaining how it all works. He knows his Father – and he gives us that knowledge. As we receive that knowledge, God's love makes its home in us, and Jesus dwells in us.

Our old nature doesn't like this gospel because it gives it no role – it is not based on human reasoning. The only part we play is to receive the knowledge of God - which is Jesus' gift to us.

Chapter 13. I No Longer Live, But Christ Lives in Me

Let's tease-out this 'knowledge of God'.

It seems that Jesus knew God in a way that the rest of the human race didn't. Jesus knew him as a man with a perfect nature - rather than one who attempts to know God through the fallen nature. The fallen nature is like a lens that we place in front of God as we attempt to view who he is – it is a lens that measures our worthiness to stand before God on the basis of our religious lifestyle and behavior. Jesus had no such lens, so all he saw was the unrelenting love that flowed from the Fathers heart to him.

For example; we often hear people saying that God blesses us because of the godly lifestyle choices we make. And conversely God can't bless us if we are living unrighteous lives. The lens of 'human behavior' adds something to the heart of God which is not actually there... *conditions!*

We take the unconditional love of God / and add conditions to it - when we attempt to understand it through the reasoning of the fallen nature. The fallen nature cannot tell God who to be, God will not remake his unconditional love just to accommodate the insecurities of the fallen nature.

Jesus knows his Father without the limitation of 'conditions'.

And that is the primary gift that he gives to us.

> *A 'conditional' understanding of God's heart is the legacy of Adam.*
> *An 'unconditional' understanding of God's heart is the legacy of Jesus.*

This 'unconditional knowledge of God' is essentially the reason why Jesus lives in us. He doesn't live in us so that we can do miracles, preach sermons, or heal the bodies and minds of broken humanity *(these are the overflow of the real reason he lives in us)* – he lives in us so that we will know the Father's heart.

And we must, *each one of us,* discover this love for ourselves - before any act of service or ministry can have real meaning. When we discover the Father's love we begin to spontaneously live great lives in the power of the Spirit – *fountains of living-water burst forth from our lives.* The unconditional love of God is at last free to be expressed, without our actions being driven by the insecurities of the fallen nature.

For most of my life I paid scant regard to 'Christ in me' – at best I thought of it as symbolic, rather than literal. I couldn't grasp the practical relevance of it - now at last I realize that *Jesus lives in me in order that the love the Father has for Jesus - may be in me.*

Everything Jesus did, and said, came from this one thing – without the Father's love he had nothing, and could do nothing. But with the Father's love, he was able to set the world free. The Father's love was the powerhouse of everything that Jesus accomplished.

> ***The Father's love was the only thing Jesus needed to know.***
> ***And it is primarily the thing that the flesh has hidden from us.***

A closer study of the book of John reveals the way Jesus operated – *what made him tick.* It reveals to us the divine operating system that enabled Jesus to do so much - it is the only operating system that actually works, and it is the operating system that we must re-discover if we are to live above the issues of life.

When Jesus said in John 16:33, "I have told you these things, so that in me you may have peace. In this world you will have trouble. But take heart! I have overcome the world." He was passing on to us his operating system – he was declaring to us another way to live.

He was saying that the only way to live above the troubles of this world is that we rest in the in-dwelling presence of the one who overcame the world. His presence in us reveals to us something that the flesh can't – *anything is possible when we grasp the unconditional love of God.*

Chapter 14
The Divine Operating System

I have written about the operating system of humanity before to illustrate the difference between the conduct of the Old Nature, and the New Nature. I would like to take the illustration further now, and examine the operating system that Jesus used – the book of John has much to reveal about it.

John had a unique understanding of how Jesus was energized and motivated by his Father's love. In fact John seems to have made it his own operating system. John is the only disciple who calls himself 'the disciple whom Jesus loved'. In John 13:23 / 19:26 / 20:2 / 21:7 / & 21:20 - John gives himself the title (*five times in total*). It is not recorded in any other gospel, so no other disciple seems to be aware of such a title – but John was aware of it because it defined his existence, *it empowered his life.*

There is no record that Jesus actually called John 'the disciple whom he loved' – in fact the only name Jesus gave to John was the name 'sons of thunder', together with his brother James in Mark 3:17. John seems to have quoined the name all by himself, because he understood that the love of Jesus was the dynamic of his life – in the same way that the Father's love was the dynamic of Jesus life.

As far as John was concerned he was the absolute object of Jesus love. He wasn't declaring that Jesus didn't love the others as well – *he was simply stating the thing that was obvious to him* – his existence was completely defined by the fact that he was hidden in the love of Jesus, it was always before him.

Jesus defined himself in much the same way:

John 3:35 'The Father loves the Son...'

John 5:20 'For the Father loves the Son...'

John 10:17 'The reason my Father loves me...'

John 15:9 'As the Father has loved me...'

John 15:10 'I remain in my Father's love.'

John 17:23 '... even as you loved me.'

John 17:26 'in order that the love you have for me may be in them.'

It is clear that Jesus was deeply conscious of his Father's love, it was always before him. It filled his screen – even during the most difficult of times, it enabled him to stand boldly against the storms of life.

> ***Jesus was empowered by his Father's unconditional love,***
> ***and we in turn are empowered by God's love expressed through Jesus.***

The work that Jesus accomplished on the cross was so much more than bearing the punishment for our sins – he also crucified the Old Nature in us, so that he could 'move-in' with his own nature, and reveal to us the heart of God. Our Old Nature had to die because it has no capacity to see the heart of God – in fact; the Old Nature came into existence as the result of humanity turning its face away from God.

The very point of Jesus crucifying our Old Nature is that we might never again fear God.

Fear is the defining characteristic of the Old Nature.

It first appeared back in Genesis 3:10 Adam answered, "I heard you in the garden, and I was *afraid*", and has been the hallmark of humanity ever since – the bible records the fearful heart of humanity, from front to back.

Angelic visitations were often prefaced with the words 'fear not'. Jesus himself often chided the disciples because of their fear.

> *Fear is the normal human condition*
> *– but it is completely out of place in the realm of the Spirit.*

1 John 4:18 tells us; "But perfect love drives out fear, because fear has to do with punishment. The one who fears is not made perfect in love." Here is the divine operating system at work – as we grasp that the perfect love of God has made us perfect too, all fear falls away, and we are carried aloft by the heart of our Heavenly Father.

If we are to operate in the way Jesus did then we must close down the 'fear-based' system of Adam and discover the restful ways of the divine realm. The defining difference between these two systems is that Adam based his access to God's favor upon his own earthly performance and behavior, whereas Jesus based his access to God's favor upon the unconditional love of his Father.

I don't believe that Jesus went about with a specific and deliberate intention of doing good, but rather that goodness just flowed naturally through him as he rested in the unconditional love of his Father – he couldn't stop 'doing good' because it was his nature. As I said earlier; it is the divine operating system at work – Jesus rested in the goodness of his Father, and goodness in his own life was a result.

> *And now the same can be said of us;*
> *true goodness is not something we do,*
> *it is something we receive from God's heart,*
> *and a life that demonstrates the visible evidence*
> *of that goodness, is the result.*

The tricky part is learning to rest in that goodness – learning to dial-down our fear-based hearts, and trust that God has us safely in his loving arms. The question that many people ask at this point is "What if God doesn't come through?" "What if I am presuming on something that God never really promised?"

It's a good question to ask because it brings us right up to the line – will we step over it and entrust our entire being into his goodness / or will we retain control, and stay on safe ground - and just hope that God will be nice to us, because we are doing our best.

There are no guarantees, as least not in the realm of human reasoning. The only guarantee we have is that God loved us so much that he sent his Son to die on our behalf – our part is to determine if that guarantee is sufficient.

Perhaps we should begin to refer to ourselves as 'the one whom Jesus loves'. John led the way for us; he showed us how to think as one who has truly been set free by the love of God – all that remains is that we leave fear behind, and actually trust that God is as good as he says he is.

Chapter 15
The Father's Heart

Earthly examples of a father's love do not adequately describe our heavenly Father's heart. When we package the heart of God into human-like emotions (only bigger and stronger), we barely scratch the surface. It's important we get this right if we are to attempt to live by the Divine Operating System.

To do this we will drill-down further into the words of Jesus found in the book of John.

It's all about 'the fear of getting it wrong'!

Before we look closer at Jesus words, let's visit 1 John 3:20 "This then is how we know that we belong to the truth, and how we set our hearts at rest in his presence whenever our hearts condemn us. For God is greater than our hearts, and he knows everything".

We set our hearts at rest, when we realize that God is greater than our hearts – and even though he knows <u>everything</u> about us, he does not condemn us.

We cannot 'get it wrong', while we believe that God will never condemn us. If we harbor fears of unworthiness to be in God's presence, then we are disagreeing with God – *(and he knows everything)* – so 'fearing God' is the only way we can get it wrong.

The term *'getting it wrong'* requires some clarification in this context.

> ***Getting it wrong is not committing sin***
> ***- it is doubting the ability of Christ's sacrifice to present***
> ***us holy before the Father.***

We must make this leap if we are to ever walk boldly and confidently as Christians. Christ did not come to condemn us, but to save us. John 3:17 says; "For God did not send his son into the world to condemn the world, but to save the world through him".

We cannot expect the favor and blessing of God to be manifest in our lives while we doubt our worthiness to receive it, if we do, then we are disagreeing with God – *because he says that Jesus has made us worthy*. So we must lift our eyes off our own inadequate lives *(which bring us into condemnation)*, and on to Christ's life which brings us freedom from condemnation.

In my experience Christendom is broken up into two groups; those who believe they are doing ok, and that God should be happy to have them on his team / and those who believe they are not ok, and God wouldn't want them on his team. My observation is that the second group is in the majority.

This majority group has failed to grasp that God has ceased scrutinizing their lives in the hope of finding redeemable qualities and goodness – God looks for one thing only, belief that Jesus did enough to destroy our unworthiness, and present us to the Father as perfect. When this belief is present we are hidden in the work of Christ, and the Father only sees the perfection of Christ in us.

Now getting back to 'the Father's heart'.

For the greater part of my life I tried to approach God clothed in my best religious activities and righteous lifestyle. But God wasn't interested in these because I didn't actually have the capacity to jump high enough in the 'Christian Lifestyle Olympics' – he just wanted me to rest in the knowledge that Jesus had jumped the bar for me. He had won the race, and handed me the victors ribbon – there was no hurdle left to jump.

I was so distracted by 'trying to please God', that it obstructed the thing I really

Chapter 15. The Father's Heart

wanted – *free and clear access to the Father's heart*. It was like a dam wall that I had inadvertently constructed, that held back the flood of God's favor and blessing – in effect I had created God in my own image (I had limited him to the rules of the Old Nature, but he wasn't in them, and couldn't be constrained by them) – *even if my insecure heart insisted on it!*

Access to the Father's heart was free; Christ had purchased that access and given it to me as a gift. It was abundant, unconditional and spontaneous – but my insecure heart put limits where there were none, it added conditions that didn't exist, and it controlled the 'free flow' which characterized God's generous nature.

So the question that confronted me was this; "Could I recalibrate my heart and mind to operate according to God's nature, not my human insecurities". It would mean that I would approach the throne of God just as Christ did – without reluctance, hesitation, fear, or unworthiness.

It would mean that I would boldly presume upon the heart of God.

Could I make the shift?

Could I think like Jesus?

Firstly; it would be necessary for me to re-embrace my original design (a man made in the image of God) - I would have to take hold of a truth that has been hidden for the ages.

In the end, the only obstacle that existed between me / and my Heavenly Father's heart – resided between my ears. I had to begin believing it was my destiny, my inheritance, and my right as a man re-born of God. I had to make such a radical shift in my thinking that I cease to regard myself as 'a man reaching out to God', and begin regarding myself as 'a man who is permanently seated in the most intimate presence of God'.

Just think of it, Ephesians 2:6 tells us that we are "<u>seated</u> with Christ in heavenly places". Even the angel Gabriel said in Luke 1:19 "I am Gabriel; I <u>stand</u> in the presence of God". Gabriel stands / and we are seated – this is the salvation that Christ has given us. This is the heart of the Father – that we would sit with him as his sons and daughters.

Secondly; I would need to come to terms with the nature of God's heart – my earthly concepts of God's heart would have to go, I would have to re-build from the ground up.

I had grown up with the view that God was a 'loving-judge'. That he had two distinct aspects to his character, and that each came into play according to the lifestyle we presented to him. God was 'loving' if we were good, and 'judging' if we were bad. Overlaid onto this 'judging' aspect of God's character, was the 'loving' part – his 'judging' was somehow motivated by his 'loving'... *it was all very confusing.*

But this thinking didn't jell with the scripture from 1 John 4:18 "But perfect love drives out fear, because fear has to do with punishment. The one who fears is not made perfect in love."

> ***It seemed that while I was concerned with God's 'judging'***
> ***– I couldn't discover the perfection contained in his 'loving'.***

So I decided to explore a radical new thought; "what if God wasn't actually a judge at all?"

What if the 'judging' part of God was a result of the Human Operating System, not the Divine Operating System?

Adam began life feeding on 'the Tree of Life' – the heart of God fed him righteousness for free, it was the way God had designed the whole thing. Then Adam decided to 'change his diet' and feed on 'the Tree of the Knowledge of Good and Evil' – he rejected God's free gift of righteousness and decided to generate righteousness himself. He decided to construct a self-made form of righteousness by his own management of 'good and evil' – and present this righteousness to God to attract God's blessing and favor.

In so doing Adam elicited from God, a response that God had not intended for man - Adam insisted that God be the judge of his life. He insisted that God

Chapter 15. The Father's Heart

respond to man according to man's self-built worth.

Adam declared - 'I won't have your love if I can't earn it'.

But did that make God into a judge?

It is clear that God judged the children of Israel in the Old Testament, it was a stern, rigid form of judgment that required absolute obedience – else suffering, and even death, might result. There was no wriggle space, holy living was required to satisfy a holy God – it wasn't enough to 'do your best', nothing less than perfection would do. It was a judging based on their Old Covenant existence.

Enter the New Covenant: is God still a judge?

Over time I had developed a 'benevolent judge' theology. God was still holy, but because Christ had died for my sins, God was now willing to accept my best efforts. God was still focused on having me live a righteous life – but now there was some wriggle space that accommodated my humanity. In other words; Christ's job was to get his Father to lower the bar.

It's strange how our Old Nature can shape our theology. I had neatly positioned God into a theology that defined him as a kind old gentleman, one who was legally obligated to judge me / but would rather wink at my imperfections if I was trying hard. I had allowed God some grey areas – as a way of rationalizing his 'loving-judging' nature.

I realize now that God cannot compromise his holiness to accommodate my weakness, and that Christ's work had nothing to do with lowering the bar. The bible is quite clear on this 'you shall be holy for I the Lord your God, am holy'.

It is obvious, that the salvation that God decided upon *before the creation of the world,* was more far-reaching than simply lowering the bar of holiness – God kept the bar at the very top setting and devised a salvation that would enable us to jump it.

This salvation involved 'the Tree of Life' (Jesus himself) – Jesus leaped over the holiness bar, and we did with him / and in him. We are hidden in him as we feed on *his* righteousness, and he carries us aloft into perfect righteousness as we rest in his work on the cross.

The Father's heart is not expressed in a salvation that reaches down to my weak human nature – it is a salvation that carries me up into God's perfect divine nature.

Christ became me – and I became Christ. Anything less than the complete reconstruction of my nature *(back to its original perfection)*, is insufficient to present us before the Father, *holy and blameless*. A salvation that retains any of my previous human condition is inadequate for such a lofty task – my spirit was born anew with the heart of God.

Adam declared; 'I won't have your love if I can't earn it' – and God responded 'you are incapable of earning it - so I will give you my nature for the second time. Christ will re-make you in my image - which will give you free access into my loving heart'.

***Now God and I have the same heart,
just like it was in the beginning.***

Chapter 16
Participating in the Divine Nature

The 'benevolent-judge' theology, that had defined my understanding of the heart of God for most of my life, didn't stand up to the closer scrutiny of my Deep Field exploration. The bigger my understanding of the scale of my salvation became, the more I became dis-satisfied with my old paradigms.

It seemed that I had contained God into earthly limits – which ultimately rendered him human-like. I knew instinctively that God was not human-like, but I could find no other way to process who he was. So I assigned to God the best of human attributes - *only magnified way out beyond the earth-based model.*

In my quest to understand God more realistically, I stumbled upon the words of Peter in his second letter 1:3; "he has given us his great and precious promises, so that through them you may participate in the divine nature"... *was Peter really suggesting that we <u>participate</u> in the Divine Nature?*

It was a line in the sand, if I stepped over it my faith could never be the same again – this was truly Deep Field stuff. It was the stuff of eternity, and the realm of the Spirit, if I crossed this line I might never return to my safe, neatly packaged, Christianity ever again.

But, what exactly is the 'Divine Nature' that Peter was referring to?

It is the loving and righteous substance of God - it is more than just holy behavior, it is the essence of who he is.

Stay with me now as I try to find words to describe the indescribable. You have been very patient so far, and this subject will call upon even greater perseverance.

I am attempting to clarify the difference between the fact that 'God expresses his character <u>out of</u> who he is / whereas man expresses character <u>to establish</u> who he is'.

The problem with assigning human-like characteristics to God, is that humanity carries character in a completely different way to God. Human character is fluid and relative; it is a part of the mix of our personality and ability. We might say that someone is patient, but that patience is limited by their unique mix of personal attributes – they might be patient with the needy, but quite impatient with others who are lazy or self-indulgent.

Every human quality has limits and triggers / God's qualities are unlimited. That is why God <u>is</u> love – he is so intrinsically connected to the characteristic of love, that if he ceased to love, he would cease to be God.

We, on the other hand, may be considered loving – but if we cease to love, we do not cease to be ourselves. We simple stop displaying a characteristic we have become known for.

It is impossible for God to 'not love'.

Yet in Romans 9:13 it says "Jacob I loved, but Esau I hated." God detested Esau, he didn't love him. Jacob and Esau were twins; they were twins who would ultimately become two nations. As the oldest son, Esau had the birthright – but he considered his birthright as worthless, and sold it for a pot of stew.

God's love was upon Jacob because he valued his family linage *(he belonged)* – but his love couldn't find a place to rest upon Esau, because Esau de-valued his family linage. It's not that God stopped being a loving God, but that Esau placed himself outside of the reach of that love by stepping away from the promise God had made to his grandfather Abraham. God said to Abraham "All the nations of the earth will be blessed through you" – but Esau de-valued the promise of God, and stepped out of the family linage of God's blessing.

Esau handed God a classic 'Adamic' response, he said to God 'I don't want your love on your terms, I want to be god of my life' – and the flow of God's love was blocked by Esau's choice.

It is the same for us today. God loves us, and has provided the means whereby we can be his sons and daughters again – the only way that love can be obstructed is if we deny our birthright.

> **God cannot stop loving us; if he did he wouldn't be God.**
> **But he won't force that love into us - we must let his love in.**

It is impossible for God to 'not be holy'.

If God ceased to be holy, he would cease to be God. It is not a virtue or characteristic that God pulls out of his array of qualities from time-to-time as required – he is intrinsically holy. He is righteousness. He is perfect goodness. It is not a tap that he turns on and off, he is inseparable from his holiness.

These divine characteristics are <u>always</u> shining forth from the heart of God – <u>they are his glory</u>. God is not like us - we are not assigned a particular characteristic unless we publicly display it. For instance; the evidence of love in our lives causes people to call us 'loving'. God is not dependent on the expression of holiness to be evident for him to be called holy, because not only does he display holiness – he is holiness.

> **As I said earlier,**
> **God does good because 'He is good'**
> **we do good, in an attempt to become good.**

When Moses asked God to show him his glory in Exodus 33:18 God said "I will cause all my goodness to pass in front of you" God's goodness, his holiness and righteousness, are his glory. So magnificent, is the perfection of God's heart, that it radiates glory.

In John 17:22 Jesus says "I have given them the glory that you gave me…" What glory did Jesus give us? He gave us the perfect and holy heart of his Father. *Christ set us free from 'the visible evidence of human effort', as the prerequisite for holiness to characterize us.*

He gave us the God kind of holiness,
it is now who we are, it is the essence of our being.

This is 'participating in the divine nature' – it is no longer characterized by what we do, but by the son-ship which is ours through Christ. Jesus returned us to the linage of God's love, righteousness and blessing – we are once again perfect sons and daughters of God by birthright, John 1:12; "We have been born of God".

That's not to say that we cease doing good, we simply do it now as the spontaneous overflow of God's nature in us.

To be 'Born of God' implies that we are made of the same holy substance as God, if it were not so we could not approach the throne of God with confidence – *the vagaries of our human attempts at righteousness are just not sufficient to present us to the Father.* Religion may have convinced us that human intensity, earnestness, and zeal in prayer and worship give us entrance to the presence of God – *but why would we bang on the door of heaven, when it is already our home.*

As I said earlier; the divine nature is the loving and righteous character of God - it is more than a personal quality, it is the essence of who he is – and now it is the essence of who we are.

This gospel of Jesus is scandalous, it defies every instinct that the Old Nature considers reasonable – we become as perfect as The Most Holy God... *for free.*

It is this distinction between the way divinity and humanity carry righteousness, which enables us to understand the issue as it related to Adam when he stepped away from God in the garden. Adam began life as a man who had the same heart as God (he was made in God's image), and while Adam remained in his union with God he was holy and perfect in the very essence of his being.

As we know, Adam opted out of this existence and chose instead to generate his own virtue. This virtue was measured by 'what he did'. If there was no virtue evident, then he could not be called virtuous. Adam had placed himself (and all of humanity) on the hamster wheel of self-generated worth – if the good deeds stopped flowing from his life, then he could not be labeled 'good'. He

Chapter 16. Participating in the Divine Nature

was stuck. Locked in a continuum of 'doing good' to have any personal worth.

In contrast, the divine nature carries righteousness in a completely different way. The divine nature does not depend on its own life of 'good deeds' to be considered righteous – it is righteous simply by being in union with the source of all righteousness, God himself.

We do not have to 'do righteousness' to be righteous – instead we receive it from the heart of God. It flows from him into us, much like water flows down a river. The end result is that the righteousness we display is actually God's righteousness flowing through us.

> ***We go to the River of Life (Jesus) and drink of his righteousness,***
> ***We are made righteous by receiving, not doing.***

My Deep Field exploration into the depth of my salvation has revealed doors previously unknown to me. This exploration has revealed a truth that is contained all through the New Testament, but previously concealed from me by my Old Nature "I am primarily a spirit, living in the kingdom of God, with the divine nature as the deep essence of my being".

I will never again enter any faith-doorway as a mere man seeking God – I will always approach God as one who is hidden in his divine and holy nature, *a man already 'found in God'.*

Chapter 17
Seeing the World as God Sees It

There are many verses in the bible that tell us about God's objective in sending Christ to earth:-

1 John 3:5 "But you know that he appeared so that he might take away our sins."

1 John 3:8 "The reason the Son of God appeared was to destroy the devil's work."

John 10:10 "I have come that they may have life, and have it to the full."

If we combine these three verses it might read like this; "Christ came to destroy the devil's work and take away our sins – this released the full life of God into our hearts."

These verses and others like them spell out the purpose of Christ's life and death; they articulate with clarity what he had in mind in coming to earth. But was Jesus successful in his work? Did he achieve the outcomes that he was sent to?

Did Jesus get the job done?

Perhaps he took away the sins we committed prior to salvation / but none that we have committed since. Perhaps he destroyed the devil's work up until we were saved / but left us to battle with him after he went back to heaven. Perhaps he gives us life...*as long as we are doing the right thing.*

This would mean that he only got part of his job done, and left us with the task of mopping-up until we join him in glory.

If, on the other hand, he was completely successful in his mission – then all of our sins are gone, the devil's work has been destroyed, and we have been filled with the life of God.

We human beings, tend to view the success of Christ's mission through the evidence of perfect order and harmony in our earthly circumstances. We reflect on our ongoing failings, the apparent activities of the devil, and the meager measure of abundance in our lives – and determine that Jesus may have been successful 'in-principle', but 'in-practice' it's a bit hard to see. So we consider the success of Jesus mission as an 'eternal' success, but not particularly evident in the 'here and now'.

What about the Father, what does he see?

Does he see that the work of Christ is not gaining the traction that he would have liked - so Christ was really only partly successful in his mission? Does he look at the lingering frailties and failings of life on earth and lament that Christ did his best – but not a perfect score? Ten out of ten for effort - but only six out of ten for results.

Or maybe the Father is so fully informed of the staggering accomplishments of the blood of Christ, that as far as he is concerned Christ has destroyed the work of the devil, and our sins as well, and that his divine life is flooding the hearts of believers without measure.

Perhaps when Jesus made his final declaration on the cross "It is finished" he meant that the job he had come to complete was finished, the reign of satan was finished, our sins were finished, and the filling up of the hearts of men with the life of God, was finished.

Were it not so, Jesus would have limped back to heaven as a wounded soldier who lived to tell the tale, but didn't liberate the captives. The Father did not disagree with Jesus declaration; he didn't say "it's not quite finished Son, there's still a lot of water to go under the bridge".

Instead Jesus returned as the triumphant and victorious one. Colossians 2:15

says "And having disarmed the powers and authorities, he made a public spectacle of them, triumphing over them by the cross."

If we are to get our heads around the perspective of our Heavenly Father, and begin to see as he sees, we must determine once and for all if Jesus was successful in his mission. Not partially successful, or mostly successful, or even successful 'in-principle' – we must determine if he was 100 percent successful as it relates to us personally.

Did he destroy the devil (as far as I am concerned), did he remove sin from me (all sin), and did he fill my heart full of his own divine, eternal life?

If we are reluctant to step over that line
– then we will never see the world as God sees it.

I am not talking about an academic agreement here; I am saying that this must be our conviction for every aspect of our existence on planet earth... and that we stake our very lives on it.

Christ did the job – and I am the proof.

Certainly not the proof that my life is now free of earthly difficulties and circumstances, but proof that the Father is so fully informed of the magnitude of Christ's work in me, that it is impossible for him to view me apart from Christ – *when he sees me, he sees Jesus.*

Christ was so successful in his mission, that I cease to exist as an individual, I am now lost forever in the stunning accomplishments of his blood. The world may continue to broadcast its message about who I am, and what I amount to *(or don't amount to)*, but the blood of Christ speaks so clearly that *'I have been made righteous'* – that the earthly broadcast never actually reaches the Fathers ears.

The only proof that the Father needs, is the blood of Christ.

In Ephesians 5:25 Paul describes the work that Christ undertook "Christ loved the church and gave himself up for her to make her holy, cleansing her by the washing with water through the word, and to present her to himself as a radiant church, without stain or wrinkle or any other blemish, but holy and blameless."

The only thing that stands between the 'theoretical' and the 'reality' of this statement *is whether we believe it*. Paul states clearly Christ's intention in coming – and now it is up to us to decide if he was successful.

If we can decide that the 'word of God' is superior to the 'evidence of the flesh', then we can begin to see the world as God sees it. It all comes down to 'what we choose to believe'.

The obstacle to overcome is that we automatically expect the natural evidence to agree with God's perspective. We think that if it is evidenced on the ground – then it is also recognized to be true in the mind of God.

But that is not the case; God sees an entirely different reality to the one that we see with our natural eyes. He sees a world so completely transformed by the blood of Christ that the earthbound evidence is completely lost from view, the stunning transformation wrought by the blood of Christ fills the Father's heart – *all that remains is that we see it too, and live as the transformed ones.*

Chapter 18
Living in Eternity, While on Earth

As I began to read through the books of John *(on the look-out for the deeper spiritual information that I had missed)*, my whole understanding of 'eternal life' and 'eternity' started to unravel – things I had considered to be set-in-stone began to look less certain.

Eternity had always been about a 'place', and eternal life was my existence in that place. The place was heaven, and I went there when I died.

John 17:3 says "Now this is eternal life: that they know you, the only true God, and Jesus Christ, whom you have sent".

And 1 John 1:2 adds, "And this is the life that was revealed; we have seen it and testified to it, and we proclaim to you the eternal life that was with the Father and was revealed to us".

And finally John 5:24 says; "Very truly I tell you, whoever hears my word and believes him who sent me has eternal life and will not be judged but has crossed over from death to life".

John seemed to be saying something different to my previous understanding – eternal life is not about a place, but a person (his name is Jesus). It is not a location, but a spiritual knowledge.

I do not 'go there' when I die,
- but I 'have it' when I believe.

This jelled with the verse in John 1:4 "In him was life". John didn't separate Christ / and eternal life – as far as John was concerned, they were the same thing. I had previously separated them by assigning Jesus the task of giving me eternal life, and the destination of eternal life was the outcome of that gift.

But John didn't see it that way – as far as he was concerned 'Jesus was both the *means* and the *outcome*.' Jesus not only provided the way, he was also the destination.

Jesus objective was not to get me into heaven, but to get me into God.

He dwelt in heaven, so I automatically landed there too – but that was not the point of it all, the point was that I "be hidden with Christ, in God" Colossians 3:3.

This objective of 'getting me into God' was not limited to the 'after-life' – it began in the very instant that I believed... *I crossed-over into life.* It is no more real after I die than it is right now, my physical eyes do not see it, but the eyes of my heart (the believing part of me) has a clear view of this new life – it is the real me.

God does not have a second installment in place awaiting my departure from planet earth, he gave me that whole package when I believed (I *crossed over* at that time) – I just need to re-train my heart to the reality of it. This does not diminish the magnificence of the eternal existence we will share with God after we die, but rather it magnifies the amazing scale of the salvation that we possess right now.

Our existence on planet earth is not a probationary period to determine our qualification to graduate to eternal life when we die - quite the contrary; there is no difference at all between now and then, but for our ability to see it.

> *We are every bit citizens of heaven,*
> *joint heirs with Christ,*
> *and seated with him in glory <u>right now</u>,*
> *just as if we had already died and gone to heaven.*

Chapter 18. Living in Eternity, While on Earth

Our Heavenly Father is not counting the days, eagerly anticipating the moment when we will pass through the pearly gates and at last be properly introduced. He is not looking forward to our celestial reunion – as far as he is concerned we were completely reunited when we first believed that the blood of Christ had purchased us out of the kingdom of darkness.

At our death we will take off our earth glasses and see with clarity that which was ours all along - but that clarity of sight does not make the truth of our eternal life any more real. It is as real now as it ever will be, so we might as well get used to it and begin living that way.

In short; God doesn't have any more up his sleeve, we have the whole package - whether we grasp the reality of it in the 'here and now' / or in the 'sweet by and by' is up to us. But why would we delay partaking of such a staggering inheritance... *when it is ours for the taking today.*

The physical realm has a great capacity to clamor for our attention; we come into the Christian faith without the ability to see beyond the physical, and into the deeper reality of the realm of the spirit. Yet the spiritual realm is where our true existence is. If we are to live in our true inheritance as sons and daughters of God, we must avert our eyes away from the claims and clutter of the natural realm, and learn to see truth as Christ did.

The natural realm will declare that eternity lays way off into the future; the realm of the spirit declares we are living in eternity now – God will not force us to believe him, he simply offers us eternal life *and dares us to take it.*

John said in John 17:3 "eternal life is knowing God". Such knowledge eluded me for the better part of my adult life, 'how can anyone really know God?' It wasn't until I began to explore my salvation afresh that I discovered that this knowledge is not really very complicated at all, I just had to swing my gaze across to 'Christ and him crucified' and my knowledge of God sprang to life.

Christ gives me the knowledge of God, it is why he came.

Chapter 19
God Is My Home

Have you ever wondered where the human instincts of patriotism, nostalgia and home-sickness come from? They are such strong drives which are built so deeply into our being, that there must be a fundamental element in our make-up that causes them to be there.

This longing for home is inside us all, it is one of our deepest emotions. It is part of the human DNA - so intrinsically wired into us that we consider it normal.

> *Yet I wonder if there is a spiritual origin to this 'homing' instinct,*
> *which is like the natural instinct,*
> *but instead it longs for its eternal home.*

King David expressed his longing for the presence of God powerfully in Psalm 84:2 "My soul yearns, even faints, for the courts of the LORD; my heart and my flesh cry out for the living God."

There is no doubt that David was a great poet and word-smith, but his longing seems to go beyond well-chosen language to be the very deepest expression of his heart. God said of David in 1 Samuel 13:14 "the Lord sought a man after his own heart". There is much conjecture about what it was about David that caused the Lord to say such a thing - in my view David was drawn to God much like the earth's gravity pulls objects towards itself. David couldn't help himself he was a man out of control, his entire being longed and yearned for the Lord.

He seemed to have discovered the same thing as the apostle John 'he was the one that God loved' – and it filled his being to overflowing. He had seen the splendor and love that flowed from God's heart and was consumed by home-sickness for the Lord.

The apostle Paul picks up this theme in 2 Corinthians 5:6 when he speaks of being 'at home' with the Lord, and the apostle John as well in john 14:24 "My Father will love him, and we will come to him and make our home with him".

In Romans 11:36 we read "For from him and through him and to him are all things", and again in Colossians 1:16 "For in him all things were created: things in heaven and on earth, visible and invisible, whether thrones or powers or rulers or authorities; all things have been created through him and for him."

> ***These verses speak of the order of things***
> ***– everything is contained in God, and for God.***
> ***God does not live in heaven – heaven is found in God.***

When we approach our eternal home with this new understanding, we find ourselves longing for him, rather than the place where he lives.

Psalm 90:1 reads "Lord <u>you</u> have been our dwelling place" – *we will dwell for eternity 'in God'* - not only with him, <u>but also in him</u>.

It is yet another one of the mind-bending concepts that confront us as we take a Deep Field exploration into who God is... *we find that at the end of everything there is God.* He is more than the king of his kingdom; he is the beginning - before there even was a kingdom. The prophet Daniel referred to God as 'The Ancient of Days' – he existed before everything, even heaven is the product of his all-powerful word.

In Matthew 24:35 and also Luke 21:33 we read; "Heaven and earth will pass away, but my words will not pass away." If heaven is to ultimately pass away... and we are there, one might wonder - *what is to become of us?"*

But God is our eternal dwelling place - when heaven is done-with we will still be in God. This is the vastness of God, he is bigger than all of heaven, the

Chapter 19. God Is My Home

earth, and the universe combined – and we are found in him.

It is interesting that God says that 'his words' will not pass away – Jesus is the 'Word of God', and we are hidden <u>with Christ</u> <u>in God</u> – Colossians 3:3.

The bible often refers to the things of this earthly life as a 'shadow' or 'type' of the greater reality which exists in heaven. Such things as the temple, marriage, the priesthood are all examples of something earthly - which is but a shadow of the real thing in heaven.

These things are all a copy of the heavenly model which has been draped onto the flesh. The original is perfect in every way; the copy is constrained within the limitations of humanity. The original is always better and more authentic than the copy. Just as a man's shadow is but a poor image of the man, so the earthly copy is but a poor version of the heavenly reality.

Our mistake is that we take the earthly model and attempt to constrain the heavenly original within its limitations. We liken the temple of God to the temple in Jerusalem, or to the physical embodiment of God is us – but we fail to grasp the scale of the original when we view it on the basis of the earthly copy.

The same applies when we attempt to understand 'God as our home' - from the earthly model of human dwelling places. God was 'home' before any earthly abode was fashioned, and before patriotism, nostalgia and home-sickness had any expression in the hearts of men and women.

But our longing for God has been lost in the clutter of busy Christianity; our yearning for him has been replaced with programs and causes, and we no longer 'faint' for the courts of the Lord – *we just get exhausted from doing religion.*

When was the last time a Christian brother or sister was heard to say that their soul longs and even faints for the courts of the Lord? – we would look at them sideways if they did, and steer a wide berth of them. Yet this is the kind of person that the Lord says 'is a man or woman after his own heart'. Not that we become expert worshippers… *but that we lose all of our human ambitions - that we might simply be hidden in his love.*

So if we look beyond the earthly examples of 'home' to discover the real meaning of 'God as our dwelling place' – what do we see?

We see that we belong 'in God' and that all of our spiritual origins and history are found in him. We feel incomplete and lost when we can't find him, and that no worldly pursuit (no matter how religious or altruistic) can satisfy us. We hunger for God, because deep down our spirit recalls an ancient memory "we have been created to feed on his love".

Not 'do for him' - but feed on him.

Everything on this earth is 'utterly meaningless' as Solomon so aptly put it in Ecclesiastes – because we were not designed to satisfy our soul on the meager diet of humanities self-made worth, but on the lavish banquet of our Heavenly Father's unconditional and immeasurable love.

It is where we belong, it is our home, and it is the characteristic of our human design that sets us apart - we are born out of God's love, and no earthly shadow or copy of it, can take its place in our hearts.

When my wife and I return to our earthly home after an absence of time, we feel filled-up, we feel satisfied, and we feel at peace just to be home. Our earthly home has such a wonderful capacity to fill us with joy and delight – but imagine the joy, the wonder, and the delight of finally entering our eternal rest in our spiritual home... *God himself.*

Others may be satisfied with the notion of 'going to heaven' when they die. They might find some sort of comfort in joining the celestial choir, or perhaps fellowshipping forever with the great congregation of believers – I can never again be satisfied with this as my eternal destiny, it is too much the product of the flesh imposing its 'earthly shadow' over the heavenly reality.

I will be forever 'hidden with Christ in God' – it is my eternal future, and it began when I looked into my loving saviors eyes and said 'yes, I would like to go home with you'.

Chapter 20
A Marriage Made in Heaven

Ok, before we get started – don't immediately think of this as just a <u>wedding</u> ceremony, it's a <u>marriage</u> – (but not a marriage that can be understood fully through its earthly copy).

Let's go way out there and get a truly Deep Field view of this; Revelations 21:2 says "I saw the holy city, the new Jerusalem, <u>coming down out of heaven from God</u>, prepared as a bride beautifully dressed for her husband".

This scripture is reminiscent of Colossians 3:3 "We are hidden with Christ <u>in God</u>".

The holy city *(the habitation of those made holy by the blood of Christ)* came down out of heaven from God. This vast congregation of believers was in God – and they were a beautiful bride for Christ. Revelations 21:9 says "Come I will show you the bride, the wife of the lamb". The lamb is Christ, and the bride *(those he made perfect by his blood)*... are us.

In Ephesians 5:25 Paul begins talking about earthly marriage and ends up talking about spiritual marriage. "Husbands love your wives, just as Christ loved the church and gave himself for her to make her holy, cleansing her by the washing with water through the word, and <u>to present her to himself</u> as a radiant church, without stain or wrinkle or any other blemish, but holy and blameless".

Christ made us holy and perfect, as a present to himself.

If we think of ourselves in heaven as part of the celestial choir only, then we see ourselves as onlookers / or at best wedding guests, at the great divine marriage – *but we are the radiant bride of Christ, made perfect for him by his own gift of life.*

The proximity with God that the two scriptures above refer to, is a spiritual proximity not a physical one. We are not located in God's body, but in his spirit. We can see a physical body with our natural eyes, but we can't see a spirit – so we are inclined to imagine a union that has a physical dimension to it.

In Mark 10:8 the earthly model of marriage is described in this way "That is why a man leaves his father and mother and is united to his wife, and they become <u>one flesh</u>". In contrast 1 Corinthians 6:17 describes the spiritual model "But he who is joined to the Lord becomes <u>one spirit</u> with him".

The earthly model of marriage is but a shadow of the spiritual model. If we attempt to understand the spiritual model by imposing the limitations of the earthly model over it, then we seriously limit the scale and wonder of our union with Christ.

Paul also picks up this theme in Ephesians 5:31-32 as he moves from the earthly model to the spiritual "For this reason a man shall leave his father and mother and be joined to his wife, and the two shall become one flesh. This mystery is great; but I am speaking with reference to Christ and the church".

Paul starts with the physical model and then adds a seemingly out-of-place conclusion; 'there is a great and mysterious union between Christ and the church'. Paul seemed to be so aware of the realm of the spirit, that he could transition his thinking from the earthly / to the spiritual without missing a beat.

I love the way that Paul employs the word 'mystery' in his letters. It comes up often as he refers to 'Christ in us' – he seems to be saying that the spiritual union we have with God cannot be grasped by simply taking the physical model and adding to it, rather it is a mystery that we have no earthly counterpart to compare it to. It goes way beyond any earthly imagery – so it is a 'mystery' if we attempt to understand it by that means.

CHAPTER 20. A MARRIAGE MADE IN HEAVEN

So how do we understand a 'mystery' that exceeds any comparative earthly equivalent? *No small task.*

The earthly model seems so real, that we find it hard to imagine the spiritual version as having an even greater reality. It's interesting that many who have experienced a physical death and then been revived, often refer to the spiritual realm as 'more real' than the physical realm – *even without the physical substance.*

The spiritual realm contains a vitality and reality that we don't normally perceive – but it is actually far more real than its earthly shadow. King David must have perceived the greater reality of the spiritual realm, as his heart longed and yearned for the courts of the Lord. I have read that those who have died and been revived also often retain a powerful emotion for the spiritual realm – at times weeping with longing for the realm of God that they visited for just a short time.

The mystery can only be understood if we grasp the heart of God in initially creating the human race. Unfortunately our ability to do that has effectively been lost as fallen humanity has made God in its own image, through the means of systemized religion. We don't instinctively 'get the heart of God' when we attempt to understand it via the protocols and processes of the institution – we can only 'get the heart of God' when we individually make our own pilgrimage to the cross.

By-and-large we Christians don't linger at the cross of Christ, we don't contemplate its profound work, but rather give it a polite nod and get on with doing religion *(which makes us feel more comfortable).*

So if we strip away all of the man-based purposes and reasons for 'God making humanity', what have we got left? If we remove all of our responses to God; 'the great commission, the causes of the poor and needy, religious service and piety'- what is there left which can explain God's heart in making us.

Bear in mind that when God created Adam and Eve there was no commission or cause or religion – there was just God and man, living together in beautiful union and harmony.

The Surpassing Greatness Of Christ

The cross of Christ is exactly the same expression of the heart of God to fallen humanity – as the initial creation of pre-sin humanity back in the Garden of Eden. God expressed his heart in these two events in exactly the same way – in the first event he made man in his own image / and in the second event he re-made man in his own image.

So we must take a fresh look at the work of the cross to understand God's heart in creating humanity.

We read earlier in Ephesians 5:25 that <u>Christ loved the church</u> and gave himself up for her to make her holy… and in verse 27; he did this to present her to himself as <u>a radiant church</u>, holy and blameless. In 2 Corinthians 11:2 Paul says to the Corinthian believers "I promised you to one husband, to Christ…" so it is clear that <u>the church, and the bride, are one and the same</u> – and that they are the universal gathering of believers from every nation, and time in history.

In this modern world of self-interest it is difficult to understand the motivation behind Christ's sacrifice. We read in Hebrews 12:2 "Let us fix our eyes on Jesus, the author and perfecter of our faith, who for the joy set before him endured the cross…" There was a joy that lay ahead - that Jesus had locked-on to, and that joy enabled him to endure the cross.

> ***I believe that the joy that lay ahead of Jesus was his marriage to his radiant bride.***

But what exactly is this marriage, and how does it fit into the spiritual context?

The earthly copy of marriage falls way short of describing the heavenly model. For starters; the bride is the vast collection of all those redeemed through the ages, the bride has no inherent radiance but for the radiance she receives from the groom, and the eternal nature of this marriage implies that it has existed in God's heart before time began.

Mind blowing stuff!

I find it easiest to start with the eternal model, and try to understand exactly what the original was - which God used as a shadow upon which the physical was based. *We can't understand the nature of a human being by studying it's shadow - but we can understand a shadow if we know the person casting it.*

The kind of union that exists in God is different to the one on earth. The earthly model is fragile; it depends on frequent maintenance, quality time, and regular bonding. Our earthly relationships drift apart, marriages end in divorce, and loneliness abounds... *the heavenly model is far above such limitations.*

In God, the substance of the union is based on just one thing – his love. It was the same at creation, and also the same at the cross of Christ – both of these events were expressions of God's love.

God's love doesn't change, it doesn't diminish based on circumstances, or react to unfaithfulness or neglect – because it springs from who God is, HE IS LOVE. This 'God kind of love' brings a level of protection to the relationship that does not have an earthly equivalent - **God loves forever, without change, and without even the smallest degree of reaction to the behavior of the recipient** *(us)*. **His love has nothing to do with us - and everything to do with himself.**

Chapter 21
Learning How to be Loved by God

Question: Would Jesus still have gone to the cross, even if nobody wanted his salvation?

At the heart of this question is our tendency to see the actions of God in proportion to the responses of humanity. But God is not motivated by the hope that man will get his act together if given the chance, he is motivated by fact that at the very core of his own being is love – and if that love is not expressed, then he isn't God.

'Christ died while we were yet sinners'… because at the very core of his being was his Father's heart. His sacrifice was the expression of his Father's love – and if that love wasn't expressed, then he wasn't the Son of God.

God loves us whether we like it or not, whether we want it or not, whether we ever grasp his love for what it is / or not. We cannot escape his love, we are trapped in it – no act of rejection, rebellion or animosity can snuff-out the continual flow of this love.

It is like a flooding river of love,
flowing out from the heart of God for all eternity.
God can't help himself, he must love us!
He is just as trapped as we are… and he changes not.

But I must add a disclaimer:

There are many who associate God with the notion of 'a positive energy' or perhaps 'a loving force that affects us all'. Labels such as 'the Universe' and the 'sacred belonging' are appearing, as humanity attempts to resolve the essence of God. But God is not a positive or loving influence that will eventually overtake the resistance of humanity; he is The Most High God who loves from the essence of his being.

God is so much more than a universal force of goodness and love, he does not exist as the grand dynamic that is woven through everyone and everything – quite the contrary, he is very much a unique being, he is a spirit, and he is above all created things both natural and spiritual.

It's important that we get this right because our understanding of both creation, and the cross, will be skewed otherwise.

In eternity we will meet God face to face *(with the face of spirits that is)* - a 'positive energy' does not have that kind of personal connection, only a very individual God has that capacity.

Now, getting back to the reason why Jesus went to the cross... *"For the joy that lay before him".* There is something about humanity that Jesus finds irresistible; but it's not our appearance, or our good deeds, or our religious lives – he is irresistibly drawn to the heart of God he sees within us.

God made mankind and breathed his own perfect Spirit into us, and then when Jesus saved us, he breathed God's Spirit into us for a second time - John 20:22 "And with that he breathed on them and said, Receive the Holy Spirit".

This was one of the final acts that Jesus did before returning to heaven – he gave us the Spirit of God again.

We are the walking, talking, embodiment of the Spirit of God. God didn't just give us the 'left-overs' after He and his Son had had their fill of the Holy Spirit, He didn't give us a watered-down version of the Spirit of the Most High God – he gave us the most pure, undiluted, overflowing Spirit from his own heart... so that we could be the bride that would complete his Son's joy.

The Old Testament story of Hosea presents a direct comparison between unfaithful humanity and adulterous Gomer – God directs Hosea to take the prostitute Gomer as his wife. As the book unfolds God uses the illustration of the marriage of Hosea and Gomer as an allegory of the marriage between Christ and us. Gomer is likened to the nation of Israel, who God says 'were led astray by a spirit of prostitution'. Then in chapter 6, verse 7 he says 'Like Adam they have broken the covenant, they were unfaithful to me there'.

In Adam's choice to be independent from God, he was actually breaking the covenant of heavenly marriage that they shared – Adam divorced himself from God.

As the story unfolds we read in chapter 14, verse 4 "I will heal their waywardness and love them freely" and then in verse 8 "I am like a green pine tree; your fruitfulness comes from me". God heals us of our wayward sinful nature, and loves us freely - we can then bear the fruit of his love from his Spirit within us.

The book of Hosea in the Old Testament has the same perspective as the book of John in the New Testament – they both present a viewpoint from God's perspective. The motivation of the heart of God is the whole point, and mankind's response is irrelevant without an understanding of it.

As we attempt to understand the heart of God from the perspective of the earthly model we conclude that God has given us his righteousness to make us better people – but this view is a gross limitation of his motivation. God actually gave us his righteousness so that we could be part of himself again.

God wants us to have his divinity / not to improve our humanity.

Please don't be put-off by that statement; it is not intended to diminish or devalue the sacredness of God, but to reveal the scale of his love for us - that we should become partakers of his sacred nature.

And when we finally 'get that', we realize at last that our time on planet earth is simply the overflow of God's greater desire that we be 'hidden in his love' for all eternity.

The scale of the sacrifice of Christ; his life, death, and resurrection are a stunning accomplishment that has no comparison in history / but in the heart of

Jesus, they too are simply the overflow of the magnificence of the eternal love relationship he shares with his Father.

> ***Jesus does not define himself by his earthly work
> – he defines himself by his love union with his Father.***

Jesus has instinctively lived within this love union forever; we however must re-learn the unforced rhythms of it, by learning again how to be secure in the love of God.

To do this we must re-calibrate our thinking so that we see ourselves primarily as people who exist as the object of God's love. It is the highest and most noble identity possible, and like Jesus it must define our existence above every endeavor – else we settle for the legacy of Adam, and are defined by our attempts to juggle 'good and evil'.

I have to admit that at this point I find myself limited in my own ability to grasp the full scale and substance of the love union I have with God. I want to express the inexpressible, and my attempts to do so seem like I am running toward an ever-expanding horizon. Every time I feel like I have caught sight of the magnificence of his stunning love for me, I find myself discovering new galaxies of love that I didn't even realize were there.

I have accepted that it is now my life's task, it is my pilgrimage into God that will continue for all my days – that I will journey further and deeper into knowing the love of God, that surpasses knowledge.

But I am content in the knowledge that my understanding of the scale of his love is not the measure of its reality for me, and to me. God loves because of who he is, and I am impossibly hidden and saturated in that love – and day-by-day I venture a little further into the wonder of it, just because I can.

This is the 'knowing God' that the book of Hebrews speaks of in chapter 8, verse 11 "No longer will a man teach his neighbor, or a man his brother, saying, 'Know the Lord', because they will all know me, from the greatest of them to the least".

We 'know him' in our spirits...*and slowly our minds catch up.*

Chapter 22
Let the Celebrations Begin

Revelation 19:7 says "For the wedding of the Lamb has come, and the bride has made herself ready. Fine linen, bright and clean, was <u>given</u> to her to wear" [Fine linen stands for the righteous deeds of the saints].

The bride is adorned in fine linen; it is a covering of righteousness given to her by Jesus. Then a clarification is added [Fine linen stands for the righteous deeds of the saints].

This scripture is reminiscent of John 6:28-29 - Then they asked him, "What must we do to do the works God requires?" Jesus answered "The work of God is this: to <u>believe</u> in the one he has sent".

The fine linen that adorns us is our belief in the righteousness-gift of Christ.
It is the only thing that God requires of us,
because once we believe in Christ,
his righteous life becomes ours.

Our participation then, in the wedding of the Lamb, is simply to allow him to clothe us in his garments of righteousness. Song of Songs 8:5 puts it beautifully "Who is that coming up out of the desert <u>leaning on her lover</u>?" Our only task is to lean-in to his love, to let it overtake us and overwhelm us.

Christ cannot be wed to a bride of natural form *(that is the earthly-shadow type of wedding that exists between a man and a woman)* – Christ can only be wed to a divine bride, and our part is to simply and gratefully lean-in to his gift of the divine nature.

It is perhaps the last obstacle for the well-meaning Christian to overcome – to embrace the gift of the divine nature of Christ, (even though we remain in the earthen vessels of humanity). Paul wrote of this in 2 Corinthians 4:6-7 "For God who said 'let light shine out of darkness', made his light shine in our hearts to give us the light of the knowledge of the glory of God in the face of Christ. But we have this knowledge in jars of clay to show that this all-surpassing power is from God and not us".

To look at us with natural eyes we are no better than jars made of clay, yet these jars contain the divine nature of God – our only part is to lift our eyes off the container, and fix them on the contents.

All of heaven will be present at the wedding of the Lamb; it is the most anticipated event in time and eternity. There will be hallelujahs and rejoicing, shouts of gladness and 'glory to God' – and we the bride of Christ, will be adorned in the splendor and stunning beauty of the perfection of Christ himself. We will be clothed in the pure holiness that flows from the unsearchable love of God.

Remember in Revelation 19:7 'The bride has made herself ready *(by clothing herself in the righteousness of Jesus)*' - so I say; "why wait until we get to heaven". Let's clothe ourselves in his robes of righteousness today, let's not tarry at the gates of heaven wondering if we should enter – let's take him at his word, and believe that his righteousness is laid out like a wedding dress spread out on the bed, let's put it on now and live out our days as the perfect bride of our lover Jesus.

Jesus won't mind if we clothe ourselves early, perhaps he might even get the celebrations underway as well – there would be no point holding up proceedings if the bride is ready. As far as I know, the wedding begins when the bride arrives. Sometimes she doesn't arrive early on planet earth – *but if she did there would be no delay.*

Christ is certainly ready, he has presented his bride to himself holy and blameless Ephesians 5:27 – all that remains is that we remove the garments of self-made human worthiness, and wriggle into the garment that was made for us before time began.

The perfect love and righteousness of Christ is what we were made for, and it fits us perfectly.

Revelation 21:9 "Come, I will show you the bride, the wife of the Lamb" And he carried me away in the Spirit to a mountain great and high, and showed me the Holy City, Jerusalem, coming down out of heaven from God. It shone with the glory of God, and its brilliance was like that of a precious jewel, like Jasper, clear as crystal".

This bride came down out of heaven from God, and she shone with the glory of God, and had a brilliance like precious jewels. This bride was not at all shabby; she shone with the glory of God – the glory given to her by Jesus.

We shine with the glory of God when we clothe ourselves in the free gift of righteousness presented to us by Jesus. Our magnificence as Jesus bride is as stunning as Jesus himself - *when we allow ourselves to believe that our salvation could be as good as God says it is.*

Towards the end of the bible in Revelation 22:17 we read "The Spirit and the bride say come..." The bride has joined with the Spirit of God; they speak together now as one – it is the ancient and eternal heart of God calling all of humanity into his love. The bride has taken her place in eternity and calls through the corridors of time – come and partake of the love you were made for... *come.*

It is a love that has hidden the foolish experiment of Adam in the sacrifice of Christ, and it awaits our abandon to its beauty and joy... *come.*

Religion has taught us to measure the whole 'celebration' thing; it has constrained us in its respectability and proper conduct. But celebrate we must; the life of Christ is bursting out of us – how can we contain it any longer.

But how do we celebrate? Do we dance and sing for joy? Perhaps raise our hearts in exuberant praise to God? *All of the above...* but most importantly – we clothe ourselves in the righteousness of Jesus, we put-on with great wonder and dignity the perfect nature of God which Jesus died to give us.

Our reluctance to be clothed in the divine nature does the sacrifice of Christ no honor – he didn't die that we would clothe ourselves in human humility, he died that we might grasp his extravagant gift with both hands and cast our entire being into the safety and joy of it.

1 John 3:2 says "Beloved, now we are children of God, and it is not yet revealed what we will be. But we know that, when he is revealed we will be like him, for we will see him as he is".

The full splendor of our heavenly existence has not yet been revealed to us, but we know this much; we will be like him when we see him as he is. Just as Eve was made out of Adam (God fashioned her out of his rib), she was his perfect partner who had been made from his own natural DNA. So also are we made from Christ, we have been fashioned out of his righteousness – we are partakers of his own divine DNA, and we are his perfect match for all eternity.

Religion would have us climb the ladder of self-made worth; Christ breaks all the rules in the book and gives us his own divine heart without us raising a finger to earn it.

What a day that will be when we pass out of this life and see Christ as he is… and find that we have been re-created just like him. All of the things of this world that block our view of Christ will be gone, our true nature will be revealed – we are perfect replicas of Christ, not his physical appearance – but his divine holiness and glory in us, will be on show to all… *forever*.

Strangely; this staggering transformation will hardly register in the collective consciousness of the divine realm – as far as they are concerned we have been clothed with the glory and holiness of Christ ever since the moment we first believed, we are the only ones who failed to perceive it *(because of our lack of spiritual sight)*. But God gives us an amazing choice; we can begin to 'see Christ as he is' before we die – all we need to do is re-activate the spiritual sight which Paul prayed about in Ephesians 1:18.

It is available to us now – *that's why Paul prayed that we would have it*. We can begin living as the perfect bride of Christ as soon as we like – we just need to see the magnificent scale of the transformation that Jesus completed for us... *and put it on.*

For most of my life I considered myself a lowly servant of God, someone who had been given the honor of a life of unworthy servitude to my great heavenly benefactor. I then carried this thinking across to my status in eternity - I would be content to take my place in the vast choir of heaven and sing my songs of worship for all eternity. This would perhaps be a certain kind of celebration / but certainly not a very extravagant one – *considering my lowly status in the scheme of things.*

But the status of the bride is altogether different, she is central to the whole thing – she is held in a place of honor that is dramatically above the lowly status of unworthy servitude. She is attended by others who serve her needs, she does not engage in any task but to lean-in to the all-encompassing love of her husband.

Does she celebrate? Indeed she does.

She celebrates as brides do, she revels in the love of her husband – it fills her being to overflowing.

She is the object of the love and desire of the greatest one in the universe and beyond, how could her heart hold-in the joy that fills her. She has been swept-up in the greatest act of love ever known to humankind. She deserves nothing more than humble servitude / but instead she has been given the greatest treasure in the world – <u>the Spirit of Jesus has made her beautiful beyond description</u>. She is a bride fit to be wed to the Prince of Glory.

This bride celebrates by putting-on, with great wonder and dignity, the perfect nature of God which Jesus died to give her.

Chapter 23
The Bride of Eternity

Eternity is much longer than history. There are no clocks to measure the passing of time, because earth time is merely a copy or shadow of our eternal existence. God designed time to mark out the course of humanity, but eternity cannot be contained within such limitations. God calls himself 'The Great I AM' – his existence is always present tense, he holds nothing over for the future, because 'HE IS' the future.

Everything is contained in God. He does not live in the universe – the universe exists in him. He is not based in heaven – heaven is found in him. All things have been made by him, and for him.

We also were created by him, and for him.
We originated in him – and we are destined for him.

God does not live in time, he lives in eternity. He reached into the predicament of humanity as a time-less being. Though Jesus constrained himself into the limitations of all that defines humanity, his Father always related to him as an eternal being. Jesus may have lived for about 3 decades as a man *who did not consider equality with God as a thing to be grasped*' – but he still remained an eternal being to his core.

As long as Jesus chose to live within the nature of his Father, he was an eternal being. Adam and Eve were the same, but they took a different path, and stepped out of the nature of God – they became a new race of beings that were trapped in time. Their existence had been book-ended between birth and death.

Jesus was never trapped in time – it had no hold over him.

Even though he submitted himself to the limitations of nature, he always defined himself according to the love union he shared with his Father. He lived within the visible realm in his humanity, and in the invisible realm in his divinity – *both at the same time*. It was the way God designed the whole thing to work.

As far as his Father was concerned – Jesus was always in eternity.

As far as God is concerned – we have also been in eternity since we have been 'in Jesus'.

We are not going there when we die; we were re-born into eternity when Jesus gave us life.

In the same way that 'eternity is bigger than time', God's perspective of us is primarily about our union with him / rather than our short-term performance on the earthly stage.

I say all of this for one reason;
'we need to begin thinking like eternal beings'.

If we approach the issues of life with the thinking of fallen humanity, then we will reap the same outcomes as fallen humanity. God does not deliver his goodies to us because we are good Christians doing our best, he doesn't treat us like cute little babies that he benevolently feeds with his milk of kindness – he has given us eternal life, so that we can live with boldness and confidence, expectantly anticipating the inheritance released by the sacrifice of Christ.

By and large Christianity has developed a hand-out mentality, we are like a social-welfare based society that go to God for our weekly distribution of his aid – but Christ gave us much more than a supply of answered prayers and requests, he gave us himself, he filled us with his Spirit, and he equipped us to live as eternal beings just like him.

Chapter 23. The Bride of Eternity

We are re-born with the very substance of God at our very core, and we partake of that substance by thinking like eternal beings.

Then we truly have the mind of Christ.

If we choose to live like cute little Christian babies with our mouths open so God can pop-in some morsel, then we will never grow into maturity. God has laid-out the banquette of his love before us so that we will, with dignity and joy, take hold of its abundance for ourselves, and share it around.

In other words; God didn't give us eternal life so that we could continue living as we did before we believed – he has set us into eternity so that we will boldly live from his love as our greatest resource.

I read today of a Christian woman who died on the operating table – she was instantly transported to the presence of Jesus. But the most remarkable, indescribable part was that she discovered herself to be 'one with Christ'. Death revealed to her an eternal truth that was concealed by her earthly perspective of things. She was then revived and her spirit returned to her body – now she understands eternity in a way that was previously hidden, and she can live as an eternal being – even though she is once again in her body.

We don't have to die to begin living this way; all we have to do is change our minds and begin thinking in agreement with God - *(as eternal beings).*

As we do this, the eternal and divine bride of Christ begins to express on the earth all which is contained within the eternal marriage we have with Christ. We bring the celebration of heaven down here as we revel in the love union that Christ has given us.

We Christians have been so pre-occupied with all the goings-on down here on planet earth that we have missed the most important part – Christ has returned us to the original design, he re-made us 'of God', and this new identity makes our earth-bound lives appear boring by comparison.

To be content with the programs and activities of our earthly Christian institutions is so ordinary, when the extravagant celebrations of our wedded bliss with Christ are ours to enjoy. Not that we abandon the Christian community we call our church home – but that we bring to it the expression of our true home; we have been joined to Jesus for all eternity.

I am not trying to get everyone pumped-up with Pentecostal enthusiasm, but I am saying that we have *already* been pumped-up to overflowing with the Spirit of Jesus – and it cannot be contained, even in the neatly packaged activities we call church.

I don't wish to give anyone offense, that is not my intention in writing in this way – but surely the wonder of our union with Christ must exceed the carefully-crafted protocols and programs of church life. We have been seated in heavenly places; it defies logic to constrain such joy into the sensibilities of piously-acceptable human behavior.

Eternity must break through into every area of our lives.

The earthly environment in which we live is simply the passing parade of human endeavor, but our spirits have already been transported to our new eternal home – all that we are, and all that we do, are expressions of 'Christ in us', his unspeakable joy must be expressed.

Wherever we go / Christ goes. Whenever we enter a room / Christ enters. Whatever need is expressed to us / Christ's love reaches out. Day-by-day he speaks to our hearts of his unfailing love for humanity, and we are the vessels of that love – once merely men and women of planet earth, now the dwelling place of the divine nature of God.

The beauty and joy of the bride of Christ overflows from 'Christ in us' out to a lost world. As we let go of earthly striving and lean-in to our new Christ-given nature, a wonderful phenomenon begins to take place – the lost and needy of the world see past our own frail human form, and are drawn to the unconditional love of Christ which is now our true self.

This is the essence of our heavenly celebrations; <u>we are beginning to let Christ be himself</u>. As we allow him to be himself, rivers of living water pour out from his heart through us – and he is able to be who he truly is; 'the one who gives us life'.

Chapter 23. The Bride of Eternity

We are beginning to learn how to step aside and allow the righteous goodness of Christ to be expressed, and all it took was that we started to think like eternal beings.

Eternal beings know just this one thing 'Christ is everything'. Paul said it; "I choose to know nothing while I am with you but Christ and him crucified' – he had made the shift in his thinking; he no longer lived, but Christ lived in him – he was an eternal being.

Paul was just an ordinary human being like you and me, just a normal man who was walking around the Spirit of the living God, 24/7... *in a human body.*

> ***He did nothing to make it so,***
> ***but to believe that it was so***
> ***– it's called 'thinking as an eternal being'.***

It is a celebration which is foreign to the earthly environment we are used to. We are used to generating our joyous response from within our own hearts – this heavenly celebration bursts forth from Christ's heart within us. Our only part is to allow him to be true to himself so that the unsearchable, indescribable joy of heaven wells-up and we too get caught-up in the rapturous ecstasy of heaven.

Chapter 24
The Surpassing Greatness of Christ

Somehow I managed to be an active Christian for about 55 years without an all-consuming revelation of the magnificence of Christ. It's quite amazing really, to spend 55 years participating at an intimate level within an organization that represents the Lord of Glory, but not actually have the penny drop - and grasp the amazing magnificence of what I was in.

But now I get it, or at least 'I am getting it'.

Sometimes when I am talking to other Christians about Jesus I sense people drifting-off, they don't seem to understand that I am talking about something a billion times better than winning the lotto – there is a disconnect; as if it is all just a great big fairy tale, or at best a hopeful ambition. I imagine people thinking that I will get over it, and calm down to a more normal and sensible state – but I won't calm down, it has been 7 years now *(yes, I am 62)* and it gets more amazing every day.

Paul said that he considered everything a loss compared to the surpassing greatness of knowing Christ Jesus his Lord... *I am starting to get it;* the 'splendor and stunning wonder of Christ' is the Christianity I was missing for most of my life.

I participated in the whole thing - except for the thing that matters most; the surpassing greatness of knowing Christ Jesus.

Even though I was an active church leader and knew all the spiritual language and rhetoric, even though I praised and worshipped with all my heart, and even though I could teach and defend the solid doctrines of Christianity – I hadn't grasped the surpassing greatness of knowing Christ, *just for its own sake*. Not as a message to preach, or a song to be sung, or a ministry to be expressed – but just for the shear wonder of knowing him... *myself*.

> **As I began to indulge myself in the discovery of knowing him, he changed from being a message - to a person.**

He ceased being 'subject matter' about which I speculated, or a 'source of blessing' to whom I prayed, and became the one in whom my entire existence was hidden. He ceased to be external to me and became my most intimate identity. Not just my comforter, or counselor, or life coach – *but the real me*.

There is no presumption or ego in that statement; I did nothing to make it so, I simply discovered that it was so - and allowed the truth of it to wash over me, and set me free.

The more I was set free, the more gob-smacked I became.

I felt like I had won the spiritual lottery of heaven; all that belonged to Jesus now belonged to me - and now the further I go into discovering the scale of my salvation, the more I am blown-away by the lavishness of Christ's heart for me. The more I discover / the more I find there is yet more to discover... *I am lost for words*.

I lived for so many years without discovering anything new about God - now I can barely go through a whole day without the love of Jesus revealing more. I thought that Christianity could be summed-up by these two statements 'Christ died for my sins' *and* 'I will be content to live a life of religion and service until I meet him when I die'.

Christ did indeed 'die for my sins' - and if that was the only door available to me, then receiving God's forgiveness was still (by far) the best way to live... but Jesus lavished upon me so much more than I ever thought possible. He showed me doors of his love that I had not encountered in all my 55 years, and it has changed me forever – my faith makes sense now, in a way that my old life of good deeds and religion couldn't.

Chapter 24. The Surpassing Greatness of Christ

I am no longer content to live out my days doing good deeds and practicing religion, I have discovered the 'pearl of great price', it was buried deep inside me all along, and I have given up all that I was before, to possess it.

Now there is one door that I come and go from every day, it is a door that enables me to live confidently and without fear "Christ has made his home in me". This revelation is the game-changer, it has taken a belief system that was external to me, and replaced it with a person who's name is Jesus - who is inside me.

I didn't know my salvation was so big, I thought the view from my back verandah was all there was to it, but God has shown me more, so much more – hidden galaxies, upon galaxies, of the grandeur of his radiant love and glory.

And it all began one day when I was at the depths of despair, and I asked God to show me Jesus – and he did.

It seems to me that God will allow us to practice religion for as long as we like. It is our legacy from Adam, and God will not force us to give it up. He gave us a free will just like Adam; he will not force his will upon us, *no matter how much we need it.* But if we empty ourselves of our reliance on our self-generated righteousness, and come to him as the helpless people we really are – then he will show us wonders that exceed our wildest dreams.

It is the same prayer that Paul prayed for the Ephesian church (and for all of us that followed) in Ephesians 1:17-19 "I keep asking that the God of our Lord Jesus Christ, the glorious Father, may give you the Spirit of wisdom and revelation so that you may know him better. I pray also that the eyes of your heart may be enlightened in order that you may know the hope to which he has called you, the riches of his glorious inheritance in the saints, and his incomparably great power for us who believe…"

Inadvertently I had prayed the same prayer as Paul… 'Show me Jesus'.

It is a prayer that I repeat often now, because the more I see Jesus, the more I realize that all my concerns are already hidden in his love for me. This simple prayer has de-constructed my old complex prayer life of requests and petitions. If I can see Jesus, I can see that I have everything – and conversely, if I can't see Jesus... then my lack is more apparent, and I must petition God to meet my needs as often as they arise.

The assurance that all of the issues of my life are hidden in the sacrifice of Christ has opened up a new way to live - rest has replaced fear, and peace has replaced anxiety.

Conclusion

As we near the end of this book I want to thank you for persisting in spite of my ineloquent and inadequate presentation of such an extraordinary salvation – *the wonder of him simply cannot be fully described in human language.*

Some of you may have also read the first and second books in this trilogy; 'Back in the Garden Again', and 'The Lie we Like Best'. My intention in writing this trilogy has been to present an 'alternative narrative', one that has been hidden through the ages by the persuasiveness of man-oriented religion.

Please don't get me wrong; I am not a church hater, on the contrary I believe the church community is an extraordinary gift which overflows from our life in Christ. The point is that Christ is not the overflow of church life / church is the overflow of Christ's life – and we must each discover Christ for ourselves, and lay hold of the life that he came to give us. Only then can church have real meaning, and without a profound revelation of 'Christ and him crucified' – church is merely religion.

I expect that most people who will read these books will have a Christian background and a general knowledge of the gospel. I identify with this group of people, because I am one of them, and yet I lacked a sense of wonder and authentic revelation of the very person that our organization represented.

I was a believer who didn't really know how to believe.

In the final analysis each one of us must make our own pilgrimage to the cross of Christ, we must each lay hold of its astounding claims for ourselves – no other person or organization can sit-in as our proxy.

These books may have given some fresh food for thought; they may have presented Jesus in a way that is even compelling and challenging – but they have missed the mark if the individual reader has not been moved to look Jesus in the eye and examine afresh his scandalous gospel.

Once we have seen Christ for who he really is, our only possible response is to say 'I want you, I want your love and your life, and I unreservedly surrender myself to your care forever'. To do anything less would defy reason.

It may seem risky to take such a radical step – but I would contend that once we see Jesus, it would be risky not to.

A good friend of mine phoned me today to share his excitement in realizing that all we need in our lives is 'done' – it is Christ's gift for the taking. His realization agrees with the words of Peter in 2 Peter 1:3 'His divine power has given us everything we need for life and godliness through our knowledge of him...'

Up until the age of fifty-five I had engaged in a form of Christianity which declared that it wasn't all 'done' – that it still required my contribution of a life of religious involvement and good deeds. I had taken the free gift of salvation, and made adjustments to it that suited my human instinct to do my part.

But the legacy of Jesus has no room within it to accommodate the legacy of Adam; they are two diametrically opposed ways to live – *(I had attempted to run them in parallel)*. I wanted these two opposing systems to work together, and in so doing I kept alive the very thing that Christ crucified.

This is the reason why I have steered away from giving too many examples and illustrations of how 'Christ in me' has played out in my life. I want people to latch-on to Jesus for themself, and not just the method that Graeme *(or anyone)* used to connect with Jesus.

Christianity is about a person / not a system.

Conclusion

The whole point of this trilogy is that we 'step over a line' and trust Jesus for ourselves because we have grasped the wonder and scale of his love for us. You may have commenced this journey because of my words, but the ultimate destination of the journey must be Christ - The Living Word. We must arrive at the point where we individually feel completely safe in him.

So in conclusion I say this to you *my reader;* consider the possibility that there is more to Jesus than meets the eye, consider that there are doorways yet to be entered which reveal a salvation so unspeakably astounding that it beggars belief, and consider that the one who made the universe has also made his home in you.

I am certain that such a view of 'Christ and him crucified' will render you speechless too – unable to describe the indescribable… *and you will be profoundly changed forever.*

Cheers, Graeme.

www.ingramcontent.com/pod-product-compliance
Lightning Source LLC
Chambersburg PA
CBHW070629300426
44113CB00010B/1709